T0129926

THE QUEST

Searching for the Real Me

STEPHEN PAUL TOLMIE

authorHOUSE®

AuthorHouse™
1663 Liberty Drive
Bloomington, IN 47403
www.authorhouse.com
Phone: 1 (800) 839-8640

© 2015 Stephen Paul Tolmie. All rights reserved.

No part of this book may be reproduced, stored in a retrieval system, or transmitted by any means without the written permission of the author.

Published by AuthorHouse   05/27/2015

ISBN: 978-1-5049-0958-7 (sc)
ISBN: 978-1-5049-0957-0 (e)

Library of Congress Control Number: 2015906868

Print information available on the last page.

Any people depicted in stock imagery provided by Thinkstock are models, and such images are being used for illustrative purposes only. Certain stock imagery © Thinkstock.

This book is printed on acid-free paper.

Because of the dynamic nature of the Internet, any web addresses or links contained in this book may have changed since publication and may no longer be valid. The views expressed in this work are solely those of the author and do not necessarily reflect the views of the publisher, and the publisher hereby disclaims any responsibility for them.

The Five Important Questions
in Understanding One's Life

WHO

WHEN

WHY

WHERE

WHAT

Dedication

I wish to dedicate this book to the two most influential women that had a major impact on my life and were my sanctuary, during many times of rough seas during a large portion of my life. They were "my rock" and "my strength"... even "my salvation" during some of the speed bumps that life had a way of throwing at me, to test my response to the situations and the ways I attempted to overcome these difficulties.

First of all... my mother, *Nellie Irene Tolmie*, who from birth was always there to protect, defend, guide and counsel me through all the many difficult times that confronted me. Without her influence in my life, I would not have become the man I am today; and have the values, mindset and determination to succeed and become all that I could be.

Secondly... my "significant other", *Wendy Jane McCarthy,* who once coming into my life showed me eternal and unconditional love. Other than a mother's love, it was something I can hold near and dear throughout my life... even after her death. Her spirit and closeness still hover over me as a veil of peace, love and comfort. What a wonderful gift I continue to receive daily from this extraordinary, special lady. Her footprint is a constant in my life's existence and journey. The one thing I always wanted in my life is to have someone who always showed she cared for me, as much as I cared for her.

In Appreciation

I wish to extend a special *Thank You* to a friend... *Yoram Snir*, for his computer talent skills and his artistic talents which are evident in the eye-catching cover for my new book.

Again, I am very fortunate to have his friendship, the time he freely gives and the talent he has for producing this special book cover design.

Thank you again Yoram, for all you have given to me in the production of this book. Again, this was the finishing "touch" required to bring my book to life!

Stephen Paul Tolmie

Acknowledgement

I have a very special friend, *Marion Broadfoot,* who has the English grammar skills and proof reading expertise, to assist me in editing, correcting any grammatical errors that exist and sometimes choosing a better, more descriptive way to replace the words I had originally used in writing this book.

I appreciate the time she has spent, her knowledge of the English language. All of this contributes to a better product being produced in the publication of my book.

Once again, sincere thanks Marion, for all you contributed in the writing of this new book.

Stephen Paul Tolmie

AN INTROSPECTIVE LOOK   by Stephen Paul Tolmie
"Introspection" is the observation and analysis of one's own mental processes and emotional states."

Prologue

This is an attempt to look inwards to try to understand what makes me tick. It's also an examination of my actions and my need to perform... not always in a good format in my younger years; and why I felt I needed to do what I did, in the situations that occurred.

In later years, it was an attempt to understand the "hows", the "whys" and the "wherefores" about who the person in this body was. Why were all these emotions or lack of emotions needed to express my pain and my anxiety? Why was I not following through with what my brain was saying? Why would my heart not allow the proper actions to be put in place with the situation at hand?

The big **WHY** is... Why am I here a this time and in this place? When will there be a good positive follow-through on my part? How will any one person best direct me to be all that I can be; rather than just "who" is in this life-form and who is coasting along, totally unprepared for the events and speed bumps that I would meet head-on. How will I be able to perform in the correct manner? How have I not been aware of the "be all" and the "end all" course of my actions that unknowingly I found myself in... time and time again? There is a famous Dutch saying... *"TOO SOON OLD; TOO LATE SMART".*

They say it is never too late to learn from life and from the mistakes you make. But for myself, I wish I could have had a better grip on both my inner feelings and my abilities to be more aware of what I was doing to myself; and not have had "hind-sight" to rationalize where I went wrong and why I didn't realize my actions would always have a "re-action"... one that I would be forced to live with... possibly for the rest of my life.

STEPHEN PAUL TOLMIE

Before I sit down to put pen to paper (so to speak), I thought I should consult a great political thinker's opinion, to set the tone for any thought or comment that might help me express my thoughts.

The great political thinker that I thought realized the most substantial thoughts on this issue up for discussion was John Stuart Mills. His thoughts were expressed in a book entitled *"Great Political Thinkers – Plato to the Present"* by William Ebenstein, who is a professor of politics at Princeton University.

The comments expressed by John Stuart Mills came from his article entitled *"On Liberty" 1859* in which he commented *"individuality is one of the elements of well-being."*

"Such being the reasons which make it imperative that human beings should be free to form opinions and to express their opinions without reserve; and such, the baneful consequences to which the intellectual and through that to the moral nature of man, unless the liberty is either conceded or asserted in spite of prohibition; let us next examine whether the same reasons do not require that men should be free to act upon their opinions to carry these out in their lives, without hindrance either physical or moral, from their fellow men, so long as it is their own risk and peril.

The human facilities of perception, judgement, discriminative feelings, mental activity and even moral preference, are exercised only in making a choice. He who does anything because it is the custom, makes no choice. He gains no practice in discerning or in desiring what is best... the moral or mental, the muscular powers are improved only in being used. He who lets the world or his own portion of it, choose his plan of life for him, has no need of any other faculty than the ape-like one of imitation. He who chooses his plan for himself, employs all his faculties."

My thoughts about what was said in the whole article, kind of indicated "one word" as the "total meaning" to be derived from these spoken words.

The "word" that came to mind was **PATTERNS**. This word indicated how we see the world, as well as the way the world works. It makes us turn a "keen eye" to the world, to examine what is to be expected and what is not to be "expected" to happen. This then, could possibly be the reason that we train ourselves to recognize and to look for "patterns", so that in our minds, we solve everything by doing just that.

There has always been a question that lurks in the back of my mind, as to what do I actually know and what do I think that I actually know?

I suppose that the correct answer to this very question would be that if I did not know that I didn't know anything about the subject in the first place, then the subject wouldn't come to the surface to even be considered in my mind's thoughts process.

In our lifetime, we will experience many an unanswered question and some will inevitably remain a mystery forever. When we are young, our instincts teach us to "read" people... from recognizing their facial expressions to the tone of voice that our ears perceive. This helps give us a fair understanding of what is happening in our life as we grow up. However, as young people it is mainly distinguishing between the good and the bad at the time of the discussion.

As we grow older, it is up to each one of us to increase our abilities to "read" these two, totally different elements; as well as add to our arsenal of understanding, in order to further live and cope in the social environment.

Living in a somewhat structured society it was often very important that we learned good survival skills, in order to keep us strong individuals. There is one skill in life that you will carry throughout your life... to learn to pick your battles; to learn when to remain calm;

to learn not be pulled into a situation that you did not want in the first place; and not to show your emotions to those that are trying to "hook" you into a situation.

This whole experience contributes to the "survival" instinct. Therefore, it is indicative to find those patterns to help us anticipate what can, or what will happen next, in our life's venture. When we are aware of what might happen next, we can then "kick-start" our defence mechanisms much earlier, than if we did not have this previous experience to draw on. The ability to use logic, good old "common sense" or even to reason the situation... is essential to our survival. We hear about "logic"... good common sense; or applying reason in our everyday lives. From a very young age, we always question "WHY" more predominately than any other question. I know in my case, my parents became very frustrated because I repeatedly asked the "WHY" question over and over. Unknown to me, I was using "logic" to their answers and if their answers didn't make sense to me, the "why" questions would continue.

I was constantly obsessed with "WHY" things happen, because deep within me, I wanted to understand how to adapt and how the answers would affect me or my surroundings. This also brings to the surface the word "INSTINCT" which had brought me this far but its very existence in my life... in all our lives... would obviously carry us throughout our lifetime.

Another of my questions concerning myself in my quest of discovering the facts about myself and my life's journey comes to mind. "Why was I here?"

The obvious/logical answer that readily come to mind is, if I was NOT here in the first place, then this question would never have to come to the surface to ever be asked of myself.

As we grow in our society... and hopefully mature, we realize that we need to memorize rules and be aware of the "accepted norms" so that we can anticipate the consequences of our actions. These simple life lessons teach us how to react in the scenario given us and hopefully will keep us from harm.

I found a simple poem which I feel at this early stage of our discussion about "who" I am; "where" I am heading in life; "why" I am here and "what" is the makeup of the person in this body to be apropos. I also question if I should be here at all. Am I a person of worth? Has my life all been a big mistake?

The questions persist and the quest continues.

HANDBOOK OF LIFE

Learn to live with what you have
Feel free to share your love
Always show others your care
Try to speak without harsh words to anyone

Seek happiness throughout your life
Solving problems helps make you strong
Heartache is a part of life
Do not be afraid to fail
Success will be your reward

Author: Stephen Paul Tolmie

It is amazing to this simple man, how these few words can bring a man to his senses and help him realize not to "over reason" the *how* and the *why* of life; but to merely use these profound words correctly. If I do, I may be rewarded with all that I may seek and hopefully will become a better person for using them throughout my life and thus perhaps gain true happiness.

THE QUEST

"Searching for the Real Me"

WHO is this person in my body? **WHY** am I here? **AM** I a person of worth? **AM** I a person who should really be here, or is it all a big mistake... and someone, somewhere put me in this particular spot and no other... that I might actually belong somewhere else?

On the surface, these all seem to be very important questions and each of them should have a logical answer or explanation about *WHAT, WHERE, and WHY...* in analyzing; even throwing some light of clarification on the subject at hand.

Now you should be able to "see" my predicament. Perhaps I may even cast some doubt on your own personal reasons for being here... or as in my case... WHY here and not somewhere else in the universe.

Let's take a look at some of these perplexing questions. They often have the appearance of causing "distress" if anyone has the time and inclination to even try in some small way, to get close to a "logical" explanation about the reality which is the whole basis to understanding this predicament.

I think one has to start at the time of birth. It is the point of "natural" beginning. Once we are here on earth, this becomes the starting point of our personal quest and soul-searching. We begin in the comfort of a parent's care and devotion to our every need. All the staples of life are laid at our feet. There is no "expectation" on our very being nor is there any focus of "concern" on our part.

We are this "little package" of total attention. All that we are asked to do is to make some small sounds of contentment; to eat when someone brings us food and to sleep (hopefully soundly) for a prescribed number of hours until the next day arrives.

Thus, we have established a "pattern"... a "routine" and day after day we go through these same motions and hopefully all is well... not only for us but for our care-givers.

Time now begins to march onward and we are no longer in this "baby" form; but are slowly developing into a young person. Male or female, we begin to see our world starting to put demands on us: *WHAT... WHEN... WHERE* we go; what do we eat; when do we sleep. Our daily pattern or routine is constantly adjusting.

We slowly go through the education process, trying to strive for that "golden ring of knowledge". As a reward, we constantly seek advancement to higher grades of education and knowledge. We become aware of a stressful "learning curve" that will be ever present throughout the remainder of our lives.

Life is now making its own demands on "how" we use our time. We become so totally aware of how this will always judge us and our purpose. The skills we may obtain... if we don't "burn out"... are becoming a total part of every day we exist.

Let's take a closer look at this period of "childhood". We now represent "a person", a "moving entity", someone to notice; not just a little "creature" freshly "hatched", who is cradled around and shown off for others to notice.

When we were "new" we often heard people utter those *ungodly goo-goo words* about us as we were cradled in our parent's arms. Once we were recognized, we were quickly dismissed as the onlookers decided there were much more interesting things to see or do with their precious time.

BUT we are people who need immediate gratification; something to give us immense pleasure, or we quickly move on, in a quest for that specific desire. The pleasure meter is ticking and onward we must in all haste move. That would seem our soul's purpose... that golden ring of pleasure and contentment.

We want to attain and hold it for whatever time period it takes to reach that utopia of possessions and desires that we so crave.

It is in this "real world" of importance, of value or that "craving desire" to possess that certain something, that we are now part of and all too soon, we realize that we too must enter this "treadmill" of QUEST. It has been inbred in us to reach or search for values to feel as if we are a "person of WORTH"; that we can show the world that we also realize the prize ring of value, possessions and power.

These are the "things" that show everyone else that we are made of "good stuff" and have been taught well about what "real" value is. It is not this thing called *"love"* ; but rather is the *"possession"* of an article of WORTH.

Is this a cold, heartless approach to life that this author has? Or is it in reality, what everyone has been "taught" and "told to search for" to be a person of *worth?* To me, this still remains the $64.00 question. Should a person not search and truly try to obtain *LOVE* and *HAPPINESS?* Or, should a person merely go with the flow and be contented with possessions, cold hard cash, and a life without feeling for his fellow man?

If we watch the news or read a paper, too often this is what is portrayed before your eyes and mind, to absorb for consideration. It is often what the world seems to revolve around is the "common place" things and not the unexpected occurrences. This is truly the reality of the world in which we live **only** we can make a change **if** we want a change to be forthcoming.

This would require a total 360 degree change to our everyday life's existence and the way in which we perceive things. Are we truly capable of this kind of magnificent change... to actually think of our brothers' or sisters' feelings and needs? Unfortunately, I feel I am a person of doubt.

There will always be this thing called *GREED*... the total desire to be in control; to have possession of and total denial of others to have the ability (even a slight glimpse) of the greedy person's happiness and total contentment with himself or herself.

This my friend, is the world of REALITY. There are a few that have all they need, want and desire; and a multitude of others who long for an item, crave for it and yes... even long to have a moment when they too can say they have had their desires fulfilled. This may be for a split second, but they were in possession of their heart's desire and happiness. This limited time frame would rekindle from time to time and memories would return over and over again.... into eternity.

Unfortunately for those "greedy" people, this is a rare occurrence and so for them, the possibility of a "once in a lifetime experience" where they are truly happy and contented, a feeling of fulfilment will not be known. "Greed" will not stop, even for a moment, to allow them to have and enjoy this wonder that has entered their world and they quickly return to that "greed" curve so quickly.

Indeed they would not even have had any inkling that "happiness" had entered their world and they did not begin to understand what had just happened. For you see, *"Greed"* does not understand happiness and contentment.

Now I will come down from my "soap-box" and get back to my main concerns. **Who** and **what** is this person in my body? **Why** am I here and not somewhere else? **Why** this location and yes... **why** in this time frame? I will try and look at my childhood from an "outsider's" point of view (if that is even possible) without any prejudging by myself.

The stages of my life, from birth until I was ready to go school were not marked by any significant "flags of delight, pleasure or real meaning" to enlighten you about any outstanding points of interest, or concern or matters to be pondered.

I went through the same illnesses, the pains, the upsets, the highs and the lows of growing up. I could compare it to a stairway. I started on the bottom step and was not yet ready to move on to the next step on the road of life's quests.

I was not ready for school when that time rolled around. Since I was born in October, it was thought that I "should" be ready and not have to wait till the following September. As it turned out... IF I had been consulted about this new experience... and IF they had really looked at my development, my daily actions and my "supposed abilities" they would have recognized that I was NOT ready for school. I was still in my own "make-believe-world" where nothing and nobody was real at all, in my current mental state.

As it turned out, I was right and they were wrong! I was infatuated with my teacher... somehow thinking of her as a secondary "mother" figure. I took comfort in knowing she was around to protect me. I often took long naps and my imagination would take over. What was happening in the real world was of no consequence to me; nor did it hold any importance because in my dreams I could escape this "school" experience.

Since it was no surprise to me at all, I failed this first attempt at school. Thoughts of a golden ring of accomplishment, the desire to please and receive praise was not forthcoming. It really didn't matter to me; but if I had the ability to comprehend what had just happened, I wonder if this would have (or should have) had an impact on my life. I was sorry for my Mom and Dad however.

My life still seemed the same. But apparently I was going to have to go through the entire experience again. However, I would be one year older and hopefully... for my parents' sake, there would be a different result. It could show my parents they hadn't raised a total turnip.
And so, the next attempt at the learning curve was to begin. This world seemed so very strange. There were people around me who were totally unknown and I was not sure if I liked the idea or not. I wasn't even sure that I liked the new environment at all. Where were my toys, my familiar surroundings, and my Mommy? In fact, my whole world wasn't here at all!

Was this also another big "mistake" on someone's part? Surely my parents must be aware about what they had done to me! With a very sad heart, I accepted this new situation and hoped it wouldn't last too terribly long!

Boy, if I had only known! There were going to be many years of education... away from my favourite surroundings... away from the people I loved. I wanted to ask for another ticket to a different universe. I was not sure this was the right one for me; and certainly not now, in my short existence here on this earth.

No doubt you are all aware that we have no control over the time, the place or the people who come into our lives... those who "count" and those who do not. Apparently, this is all "pre-arranged" by our Greater Power... our Creator... or simply by the "luck of the draw" in some cases.

I was to lucky to be in my world where there was food, shelter, people who would look after me, love me and clothe me. The dice had been rolled and apparently I won that round. Hence I was put into this "world of plenty", where my everyday existence was not an issue but rather was the "accepted norm". No one was trying to beat me up, shoot me, starve me, or work me like a "dog".

Life was good and full; it was all spread before me to examine, speculate upon and even develop that "greed mode" of desire that would soon be raising its ugly head in my direction. For the moment, I would look into this thing called "education" and see where the chips may fall. So the developmental process was opening its doors. All the weird and wonderful contents that were part of the education sphere were opening for anyone to participate in all its experiences. For my parents' sake, they suffered no shame and my second attempt was a "pass". Everything seemed happy for me; but I could not see what was terribly wonderful. I was just thankful I didn't have to go back to that place again. Alas, after a few months, the whole ordeal started again. I learned a new concept... "Summer break". Oh my! What were they even talking about?

My world seemed that everything was all right; I could play with my toys. My mother was a constant in my world; my environment didn't change on a daily basis. My father would leave for his job (I didn't understand "that" word yet). But for the most part, everything in my world was back to normal... the way it should be. I hoped it would remain because this was where I was the happiest.

Oh no!!! Summer break was over! It was back to the learning curve process. Again, there were new people, new surrounds, new environments and a "task master". This person was like the captain of a ship... up at the front of the class. He spewed words like an old preacher, while I sat there bored out of my mind, wishing to be home with my toys, my mommy, my surroundings and yes... my contentment.

As reality would have it, I had absolutely no say in the matter. I was like a "robot" already programmed to obey and to do as requested on a daily basis. This was my "new world" a place of discontent.

Somehow, I managed to stumble through this process; or perhaps the teacher was just tired of looking at my face. Consequently, grade advancement was my fate. My Mother was happy (glad someone was) and she said to me... *"Onward and upward. It's going to get better and better and in the end you will be surprised."* I did not want to let her down, so I nodded my head in agreement, even though my heart was not into this scene at all.

I did find ways to entertain myself in this school system. Knowing that Monday's were my mother's washing days, I would sneak home and spend time in my room, playing. But I was always on guard for my mom's footsteps on the staircase or hearing the sound of her steps as she moved about the house. Surprisingly, I would always appear at lunch time to hear her familiar voice saying... *"I did not hear or see you come home. You must have sneaked in when I wasn't looking."* Unfortunately, this did not happen for very long. I learned the first lesson in life. I was missed by the teacher and a call from the principal's office soon put a stop to my "adventures".

My "dream world" came crashing down, much to my amazement. I realized I could not put one over on that darn school; neither could I put one over on my Mother!

Big surprise! I was actually using my mind to try and figure out ways to avoid going to school. However, in reality, I guess this "school business" was a good thing after all. I brushed past grade 2 and grade 3; but herein lies another lesson with grade 3. I had an "old lady teacher"... something probably left over from a witch's Hallowe'en mask. Or so it appeared to my childish mind.

She looked quite "realistic" as if she could fly away on a broomstick at any given moment. However, she did have a very old Model A car that had wooden wheels. But I am getting a little ahead of myself.

In this old lady's class, we were introduced to musical instruments. One was a plastic-like flute device. We even had an old geezer music teacher whose sole job was to teach us how to play this "instrument". His accomplishment in this task would mean he had done his job well.

As a young lad, I did not like him, or the teacher; so it would not be long before there would be a confrontation! In reality, I did try to play this stupid device; but to no avail. There was absolutely nothing remotely like "music" coming forth from this "instrument"! Being the devious lad that I was, I decided to open up the back window of the third floor and pitch it out... as a definite distaste for this "flute".

Herein lies my next introduction to life's experiences. The music teacher and even the old lady teacher had no sense of "humour". She marched me behind the blackboard divider and carried a strap with her! I piped up... *"What's with the strap!"*

Very soon, I learned my first lesson or punishment from someone other than my parents, who had only ever slapped by bottom. I could readily see this was NOT going to be much fun.

So... I timed it perfectly so that when her hand was coming down with the strap, I pulled my hand away! She slapped her thigh so hard from all the anger she put into the action, there was actually a tear in her eye. "Poor Dear!" For the moment, I had won and had proven a point... *"Don't mess with this lad."* Can you guess what the next lesson was? Guess I wasn't quite as smart as I thought I was because the music teacher marched me down to the Principal's office for due punishment.

After the music teacher explained about how the teacher was handing out my punishment, only to be on the receiving end herself, I think I saw a tiny gleam in the principal's eyes as he anticipated his next act. To say it did not hurt would be a gross understatement and an outright lie as the principal smacked the strap down on both my hands several times. My hands were bright red but I would not cry for this "son of a bitch" and consequently I made things worse for myself.

I headed to the water fountain to cool my hands and help ease the red before I returned to the classroom. If the "old witch" had not smiled when I entered the room, everything would be finished! But she presented me with another silly plastic-like flute and told me to take my seat. At this point, I was mad and "war was declared!"

As I said earlier, the "old bat" had a Model A car for her transportation with those amazing spoke wheels. At recess, I decided to try and teach her a lesson not to keep fooling with me or some repercussions might happen. I let the air out of the tires! What a glorious sound I heard as the air escaped and those wooden spoke wheels rims were now sitting on the ground. At the end of the day, I would have given anything to see the look on her face when she saw she had no transportation to get home any time soon.

In all likelihood, she knew it was me; but no one had seen me and when she confronted my parents about the ordeal, I was like an angel... my head faced my accuser and I didn't even blink an eye.

My parents, being "good parents" could not believe what they were hearing and said... *"I think he already has learned his lesson about authority figures and not to try and pull fast ones with the teachers. The strapping had been a good reminder."* Being a good mother, also said that she was mad at how hard I had been strapped and would not allow this to happen again without her being present and without her permission!

WHY had I needed revenge? WHERE did this idea even come from? Did I possess a "dark side" to my brain that I was totally unaware of and WHY was it even in my mind to begin with? WHO belonged to this inner little voice inside my head, telling me to react to this event? WHEN had I even developed this revenge-thought process? WHAT did I even expect would be my gratification from this revenge?

My second lesson, although initially a little painful proved I could "outsmart" the teachers and their so-called "authority". I think this old lady must have been smarter than I had given her credit for because from then on, for the rest of the school term, she never paid real attention to me. All was well in my world. Oh yes, she really did NOT pay any attention to my music talent or lack thereof... and so I won on this front as well.

Grade 4 was a different learning curve. For the most part, I was a reasonably good student. Because this teacher looked and acted in better accord with her students, that real harmony was the rhythm of the day. I actually started to take an interest in class and was amazed that I was curious and wanted to learn. Maybe my brain was acting like a sponge and soaking up this new and interesting knowledge.

I did have a moment of "badness"... but even though slight, it was memorable. In our school system we had a class for older lads who needed "life skills" and "special instruction". There was no other place or resource to send them, so the public school system had the room and a specialized teacher to help these young men to be able to seek employment using some life skills... even though it was in a very limited capacity.

Well, here is where my "bad" side took over. I decided to play a trick on my teacher. I had been such a good boy for too long and in hind-sight it was not a thing I should have done! But the devil had a good hold on me and "made me do it". I convinced one of the slower students, who usually walked around doing "bird chirping sounds" and singing... that my teacher had asked me to ask him... to perform in our class right after recess to give a "performance" in front of the class.

Much to my amazement, he believed me and right on cue, he entered our classroom, performing at the top of his lungs, to the laughter and applause of all the students in the room. I wish I could have had a photo of my teacher's face... the horror and expressionless look was total disbelief! It could have been worth whatever the punishment might have been.

Consequently, I learned my "third" lesson in life... not to make fun of others less fortunate. For this I was truly sorry and so the strapping really did not hurt as much because I was thoroughly ashamed of myself. I decided never again to do anything like this to anyone else. Definitely it was a worthwhile lesson and one to carry throughout life's future "frontiers".

WHY had I needed to do this trick to another human being, just because I could? WHAT was I even thinking? Obviously in hindsight, I hadn't been thinking at all! WHERE did this idea come from? Was the "dark side" of my brain taking hold of my "proper" thinking processes?
WHO in hell did I think I was? WHERE had my "self-respect" disappeared? WHEN would I shape up and begin to become a better human being?

At this point in my life, I decided to settle in to this "education process" and see where the chips may fall. I had nothing to lose and possibly everything to gain! So I began in earnest, to learn and to try to be a better person. I was as amazed as my teacher was, that my improvement and skill levels advanced beyond this class and the next... to the point that I "skipped" grade 5 and was finally re-united with the students that had left me behind when I had to repeat grade 1.

Even I was pleased with my abilities and the learning curve of knowledge that I had digested and had been able to absorb into my brain, seemed to have a positive effect. Maybe, all this was not such a bad place to have to spend my time. There were rewards to be had and the world now seemed to be a better place.

I actually enjoyed the rest of my time in public school and for the most part, did not play many more "pranks" on anyone. Although I can say with all honesty that a few more "items of interest" did cross my mind and because I was curious, some of them did get played to see what the end result might be.

I will mention one more interesting item of "scheming" that I knew I just had to play out to the end. At our public school, we had what was called a "fire escape chute" installed because our school was three storeys, for everyone's protection in case of an emergency.

Now that I was in grade 8, the senior boys were given an old potato sack to down the chute, to clean it and to remove any object that might be in the way. It was really a "quick clean" system. These years, it was common for the girls to have a separate entrance than the boys.

Some "dummy" on the school board, must have had too much time on his hands and was probably paid too much. So he probably had to justify his purpose and came up with an interesting idea. Now you must realize that the "Devil" had a major hand in this scheme that I devised.

I had always wondered why it was that boys and girls entered the same "opening" in this chute; but they each exited through a different opening. This really puzzled me and so I purposed how to discover how this might happen.

After doing my job of doing the "general cleaning" of the surface of the chute I also had to remember to open the doors at the bottom to allow anyone using the "fire escape chute" easy access to the exit at the bottom end.

I decided to continue to investigate. I walked back up the chute to find the real reason the girls came out the other side. To my surprise, I discovered about half way up there was a division in the chute. The girls were told to lean to the "left" when they were coming down and the boys were told to lean to the "right" on their way down.

Now you know the rest of the story.

Surely you could see it coming... I thought it would be great fun after opening the doors for the boys at the bottom of the chute, to walk back up halfway and to place "myself" in that spot with my legs wide open, to allow the girls to go through. As I did, I gave each girl a little tap on her shoulder as she went through. Could you even imagine the blood-curdling screams? It was a wonder that I didn't lose my hearing; but bigger events were on the horizon for me to experience.

I guess my little "prank" was not looked at with good favour and laughter. Apparently the girls had no sense of humour and neither did the teacher! Yes, another life's experience awaited me in the principal's office. The familiar strapping was going to be my fate. Indeed, my hands did hurt but not one tear fell from my eyes. I was not going to give the principal the satisfaction that he had any effect on me; nor was I going to learn any particular lesson from the strapping. I think my hands had hardened a bit and the effects of the strapping didn't penetrate as deeply and soon as the ordeal was over. Thank goodness!

WHAT had driven my curiosity to the point of putting my idea into action? WHY did I even think I might have gotten away "scot-free" without any repercussions? WHEN did my brain finally kick in to realize there wouldn't even be any reaction? WHO would actually have the last laugh from my curiosity... myself or the principal handing out the punishment? WHERE was the justice in strapping versus a stern talking to, or denying privileges to have the punishment fit the crime?

The only real disappointment came with the cancellation of my job as "chute opener" and also the fun ride down the chute. This would no longer be experienced at all. I had the "distinct" pleasure of the principal standing beside me while the rest of the class practised the chute fire drill. I guess you could say that "I got what I deserved". But I was a kid and wanted to explore my curiosity. Maybe you might even have applauded my quest for the unknown. These thoughts came from my perspective and it seemed like a good idea at the time.

I was about to finish my grade-school experiences and was anticipating the summer holiday break and the freedom that it allowed me. My mind was only looking at the "present" moment; not at the future of High School, which was looming on the horizon. To my disdain, the unknown future and that "troubling word" that I hate to his very day clouded my mind... *CHANGE.*

Oh my! Summer holidays were soon over. It would now be back into that learning curve process. Again, I was faced with new people, different surroundings, a totally new environment and the biggest "change"... new teachers/taskmasters and new faces.

In the Public School system, you become familiar with the teachers who are present in the school system. You had a pretty good idea who your teacher for the new year would be. You had seen them either in the hallways, on route to your class, in the schoolyard, on work patrol or at the school assemblies.

High School was going to be totally different and it was totally unknown which male or female was to be your instructor. This whole aspect made my stomach turn. I did not like *CHANGE* and this was a big pill to swallow. This, plus the fact that now it was a 30 – 40 minute walk from home to the school. I was only a block away from the Public School but this was another change in both time to get there and in no longer being able to come home for lunch.

If parents had money, you could buy your lunch at school; but my parents could not afford this luxury. The only comments I ever heard were about "how" the lunch was on that particular day.

I was (and still am) a shy guy; so making friends was a difficult task for me. I was gifted with neither athletic ability nor outstanding scholastic skills. I was merely a simple guy who shared classes with a lot of unfamiliar faces. (*I was a small fish in a very big pond.*)

I was given a locker to store my coat and the books I would need later; I had a class schedule and the responsibility to get to the appropriate class at the appropriate time. In the Public School, you stayed in the same class and kept your books in your desk. There was a "cloakroom" in the class and a large blackboard that the teacher would use to do his or her preparation. Consequently, High School was a lot of *changes* that I had to digest. I was not even sure I wanted to be any part of this at all.

Why was I having to go through this whole process anyway? I simply could not wrap my mind around the whole procedure and it was causing me a lot of stress on a daily basis. I was constantly wondering *who* in heaven's name was in this body of mine. Should I be here or was this just another big mistake? Should I even be in this universe at all?

I was so confused and had no idea where to take my concerns. Yes, there was always my Mother; but she was the one who sent me here in the first place! Like a sheep going to the slaughter, I blindly went where I was told... no questions, no input, no road map... just go. Yes, of course I asked and the only response was that *this was the next process in my journey through life.* So I trusted my Mother and her guidance throughout my life. She had not steered me wrong and was doing the "right thing" and pointing me in the "right direction".

Still... I did not know <u>WHY</u> I was here; <u>WHO</u> I was, or <u>WHAT</u> direction I was to go.

I plodded along, always so stressed with the feeling of helplessness and concern for the "person" in my body, whose mind had not developed the use of logic or common sense to be at ease with my surroundings.

The first year of High School was mostly a blur; the subject matter was harder to understand and cope with; the instructors were more demanding of assignments that had to in on time. The content was expected to be more thought-provoking to demonstrate that I had understood the task at hand. I guess the instructor was hoping to have passed on some knowledge and that you were not remaining a *ten-watt bulb*; but was becoming a person who was starting to learn to use your brain to solve problems and issues at hand. I guess I had endured this educational process to the point that the teacher thought I was ready to move forward and face the new curriculum at this new level.

Once again, it was summer break; but I was totally unprepared for the new experience in my life: *"Summer Employment"* . What on earth did this mean? I guess the person in my body was expected to gain employment, creating money to assist my parents with the cost of clothing and next year's book supplies. I guess my life had a brand new experience. *Nothing in life was now free!*

Naturally this came as a total shock both to "my" idea of summer time "off" and having "a life of leisure". This was another dish of *reality* and needless to say I was not sure I wanted to partake of it. This was not the usual course of events this lad was having to structure around his summer life. Also, I was not willing to go down this road; but down this road I must go... on my Dad's orders... and it was to be my "fate" for the whole summer.

Still, this lad (who was still learning and investigating his "make-up") looked for summer work... cutting grass, washing cars, running errands, painting porches, sheds, garages and any and all work projects that I could master. I was doing all these jobs to keep my father "off my back" and keep harmony in my household.

I was quite shocked at the structured life that I was now experiencing. Gone was my youth... or "indifference" to what people did; what they "expected" of me and me wondering all along... *"Is this what LIFE is all about?"*

I even shocked myself that when summer "vacation" was over, I was even looking forward to going back to school. Life's "demands"... my father's expectations... were now all behind me as I plotted this new course in my second year of High School. Again (and why not?) *CHANGE*... just like a friend... was raising its ugly head and introducing me to new people, new surroundings, new environments and dealing with unknown subject matter, that may or may not be of any interest to me.

But what the heck! I still did not have any "say" about who, what, why or even where I was going. The "unknown" lay before me and at this point in the universe, it was my destiny to go blindly down another road to see where and what might develop. Maybe this year, if I'm lucky, I might discover WHO the heck I am; WHY was I here; and WHERE in the world I was going.

I thought to myself... *"Be positive! Something may come out of this whole ordeal after all. What did I have to lose. My whole world had already been turned upside down."*

Again, I was this "entity" of nothing special; nothing of real importance. I was just a fellow human in a room full of people and no one was paying any special attention to my presence. I was just "someone" filling a desk in a room. I did not know WHO... WHAT... or WHY. Was this some kind of "master plan"? But the feelings of being uncomfortable, stressed and wondering if this might be the year I might figure out "who" I was were foremost in my mind.

Look out world! It is now going to be full steam ahead... a mad dash to get to that "golden ring of promised knowledge". Hopefully I might finally figure out the vast "unknown" that the galaxy has laid on me from the beginning of my quest about *who,* and *what* was the purpose for my being here in the first place.

My quest was very quickly shattered; as the old routine of school preparation and listening to an instructor who tried to make the subject an interesting experience. Hopefully my brain had been stimulated through this experience and it would not become a time to total boredom!

Some things were now starting to become clear to me at this point in my life. I was actually paying attention... at least initially because the subject matter was of interest. But the biggest curiosity for me was the instructor's personality and his demeanour. I was trying to analyze this instructor's real "self". Was he really giving it his *"all"* in passing along the routine that was part of the school curriculum?

I was sensing a very keen difference in each and every instructor. Their very "presentation", their tone and their enthusiasm was either "right there" at the forefront or was totally absent. I had the feeling that it was *"much ado about nothing"* in the whole course matter.

At this point, I was starting to realize that I was developing mentally. I was able to equate differences in attitude, judgement and the very "right or wrong" of the teacher's ability. I was actually quite shocked at my brain's ability to do this kind of analyzing and my perception was so clear!

After all, maybe my pursuit of "WHO... WHAT... WHY" I was in this universe at this particular time and at this particular place was now going to be revealed. I needed to allow my brain to do its job of analyzing and not just take things for granted. I needed to start to "question". This then could start to make me a person of interest and maybe some day I would be able to discover if I were a person of "worth".

The road lay before me! I had only to walk down its path and hopefully take the correct route to the end to finally reach the truth I seemed to be constantly searching for. The second term was also uneventful. I struggled to achieve the required marks, hopefully to achieve a pass onto the next plateau of the learning curve.

Eventually, I hoped to see the horizon at the end of my life's quest. As I was to discover many years hence, nothing is a constant. Change was always forthcoming. There didn't seem to be too much that every stayed the same. Feelings like *Love, Death* and *Taxes* were the only constant that would be experienced. For sure two of them; but *LOVE* would and has always remained a quest throughout my life.

I have seen and experienced during my time on this earth and sadly wish I could state more... the loss of parents, special friends, a well-loved animal and the government always there and ready to ask for more money. I wish I had a more "positive" outlook on life in general; but alas, other qualities or items of interest and expression seem to elude me and therefore not even experienced.

I am getting a little ahead of myself in my personal introspection but thought that the previous comments were relevant at this juncture in my life.

Again, through the Grace of God... or good luck... or perhaps my own abilities, I achieved another successful year of High School and would be moving on because a third year was looming on the horizon.

Oh God! So-called "summer break" was now upon us. I could sense, watching my father's eyes, what was going to be expected of me .

Another summer "job" was on the horizon to help with paying for clothing and school books. With full impact of the reality, my father expected/demanded I find a job. As he said... *"Don't you realize I am paying for the roof over your head and food to put on your plate every day?"*

I said to him... *"Hey Man! That is your job! I did not ask to be here; you and Mom created me; so cut me some slack."* I very quickly learned another life lesson! The all-out force of his slap on my face created major tears and pain to my whole body. My father was a man of few words; but quick and immediate action was another learned evaluation of life's skills.

I would need to "read" his body language more accurately... just as I had to learn from the teachers. This indeed was "life" outside the school system.

Unfortunately, my father lost his job and "security" on the home-front was now gone. Panic quickly set into the household. My father had quit school in grade 9, so to quickly find new employment was going to take a lot of work... possibly even some good luck. My dad's first cousin was a foreman at a factory and heard about Dad's bad luck. He was able to offer my dad a position in the plant as a "box boy".

These were the days when a "box boy" actually lifted heavy boxes to create a column of them, ready for shipment out of the factory. At this time there was no such thing as a "forklift" to do this job; it was strictly "manual" labour. Dear old dad quit after two days, stating it was very hard work. I am sure it was; but because he had no "education" and a wife and two kids at home, this kind of work was not an option; it was his only "choice".

He came home early the second day and I remember to this very day, my mother's words to him... *"How are we going to survive and pay the bills?"* My father replied... *"I have no idea; but I will not go back to that job!"* Dear old dad was a "quitter"... only thinking about himself. Poor dear; and it is here that I lost all respect for the man. I had to watch my mother cry painful tears which tore dreadfully at my heart.

In another of life's lessons, I had been taught that "life is not a bowl of cherries"... we were now in the "pits". This was not a pleasant lesson; but nobody said that life could or would be "fair".

This new lesson brought to the forefront of my life, the *WHY... WHERE...* and *HOW...* does one handle this new stress in the household? My mother was able to get a job with minimum wage and my father actually started hunting for a job. I too was working at any and all jobs available within my limit, to assist in running the household.

My Mom also got a second job over the Christmas holidays, working at the Post Office, assisting with the heavy mail loads at this season of the year. This greatly helped with the financial expectations in the whole household.

My mother was a deeply devoted Church practitioner. She insisted that my sister and I would attend... no questions asked. As fate would have it, her heart had been in the right place and in a short time, she discovered that the church's janitor was going to retire. She was quick to ask for the job for my father and what the job would entail and what credentials would be expected, should he be considered for the job.

Me... being a "poor dumb kid", thought that our financial problems had finally been resolved thanks to Mom's good fortune and her contacts in the church. However, I was about to learn a few more "life" lessons during this whole process. I really would have my eyes opened with the impact it was going to have on my life and on our family for quite a few years to come.

A lesson in life that was indirectly given to me; but was definitely going to affect our life was that the church elders asked my Mother to sit down and figure out "to the nickel" what money (Dad's salary) would be needed for the family to be able to survive. I didn't want Dad NOT to get the job by asking for too big a salary, Mother cut daily expenses to the bone. However, she did not realize she was actually putting a nail into the family budget. This was a long-term deal and all of us would be doing without any "extras" in life because of it. The church granted my father the job... "go figure" . They were probably all laughing all the way to the bank at such a low salary they were going to be paying out for the year's employment.

At first, I thought life was rich and full... employment, family life back to normal, my job would still give money for clothes and book supplies and life could be sort of "normal".
Poor... Dumb... Naive.. Schmuck... I was! I had no idea what my father's salary was and did not know until much later in life. But we were living on a "shoe-string" salary and our life style would certainly NOT be that of the "rich and famous".

Quite the opposite. This was a hard lesson to swallow because the elders of the church had just "shafted" us and consequently lost any respect that might have been forthcoming from me.

WHY was life going to be so hard now? Was this another learning curve? WHEN would we as a family get a break? WHERE had the "good life" that we had previously experienced gone? WHAT was now to become our fate? Was it all to be just toil and hard work? WHO would step up to the plate to help our family? WHY is there so much negativity taking hold and why am I being so naive in thinking there is help just around the next corner? Is this just another "speed bump" thrown at us to see if we can handle life?

The next lesson I learned about my father's new position in the church was that he had never gone to church before; but now he would be there on a daily basis. Does this now make him a "holy man"... sorry, he was definitely far from that! And now my ability to get summer employment was out of question. Guess who "holy man" #2 was going to be?

I became dear old dad's "flunky"... do the jobs he did not like doing and now he had this "unpaid assistant" to order around. Let me give you some idea about the size of this building. It took up a whole city block; it was a massive two-storey building with at least 30 Sunday school rooms, 3 banquet halls, a large Church office, several meeting rooms, choir rooms etc. The list goes on and every space needed to be kept up to snuff.

There was also lots of grass to cut; too many windows to count that had to be cleaned both inside and out. The minister's car (his "free" car) had to be washed weekly as well as the grass at his Manse had to be tended. It was really *SAD* that this Church was so "poor" it couldn't offer a decent salary to my father and made my mother nickle and dime the salary they would agree to pay. This is "Christianity" at its worst! At this point the "church" lost all religious perspective in my mind. I wondered how people in the position of leadership in the church could be so "cold-hearted" and devoid of any feeling toward the kind of hardships they were "bestowing" on my family and our very existence in life.

I guess I was truly naive; it is and always will be about the "mighty dollar" and "getting the best bang for the buck".

Let me walk you through the jobs at hand that were expected to be completed to keep this church a "show case" for presentation to those who attended each week. Hopefully it will give you a better idea how much the elders were expecting to get, for the meagre salary that was being paid.

This job was a seven-day-a-week occurrence for my father, my mother and myself. We were there constantly after supper every night and if dad needed my mother to help with a special function, then she dropped everything to assist. Since I was finished High School by early afternoon, I was an available extra hand to also work at whatever needed attention.

The job didn't stop there. When the function was over, then we all went back up to "the beast" to tear down all the tables, stack all the chairs and straighten up. Then dad had the task of vacuuming the carpets the next day; doing a major cleaning of the hardwood flooring; along with the regular cleaning to help keep the church presentable.

If it was an evening function, then the three of us had a huge undertaking the next day. When I was done helping I still had to come home and do homework to prepare for school the next day. In reality, I had a full-time job and my extra job of schoolwork and assignments kept me busy. I'm not implying I was hard done by; but life DID suck! I looked at my fellow classmates and all the activities they were involved in enjoying... sports and inter-school competitions.

I missed the enjoyment of "free time" after school to "hang out" and just be a regular student. <u>WHY</u> was I different? <u>WHY </u>was this my option in life? <u>WHY</u> was I not a "person of worth"? Let me take you on a further walk down the road of the duties of a "church caretaker"... along with the requirements and the family involvement. The one season I really hated was *WINTER*.

I really disliked having to get out of my warm bed on a Sunday morning early, to go to the church and shovel a city block of snow away so that the "older" people could manoeuvre the sidewalk safely and with minimal difficulty. I said to my mother... *"If the old folks want to go there, let them get there the best way they can. Who made them special in the first place?"*

My mother got very emotional and said I shouldn't talk like that. She said... *"it was part of your dad's job to see it was done and he needed help and to please mind my mouth."* I was sorry I made her upset; but my father's lack of education and only thinking about himself really made me mad. He put himself in this predicament; maybe he should work it out the best way he could. I finally realized that I was not in total control of *anything* in this environment at all!

I remember reading a comment that put all this in perspective for me: *"Tomorrow is a mystical land where 99% of all human productivity and achievement is stored!"* Hopefully, in my lifetime, things would improve for the better.

My father was busy at another big job while I was doing the snow shovelling. Because the church was heated with coal, dad had to remove the "clinkers" and add new coal to get the church heated up to make it comfortable for the older people at service time. We couldn't let these "old dears" catch a chill while they were waiting for the service to begin.

Then it was back home to get ready for church and have our breakfast so we could move into the next phase of the day. There was so much "behind the scenes" work for the caretaker and his family. Once church was over and everyone left the building having listened to the sermon, I guess they had done their "good deed" and could "feel holy" for another week.

But for those of us left behind, our day was just beginning. I would have to polish the brass plates and put them safely away. Mother was busy polishing the minister's pulpit, the brass light fixtures and then running a vacuum in the choir section.

Dad was down stairs checking on the coal furnace to make sure there was enough heat to keep the church at a comfortable temperature.

I was in the elevator because I had to mop the floor and run a rag around the wall surface to remove fingerprints and overall, just to make the place sparkle. Then it would be out to the kitchen to empty the coffee urns from the morning coffee break, after the service and then do a temporary kitchen clean up. It would all get a thorough cleaning after we came back later after our own lunch.

By now dear old dad was ready to go home for lunch so we were all homeward bound. We probably took less than an hour to change our clothes to do the through cleaning job that lay before us and have a very quick lunch to help fortify us to go back to work.

Arriving back at the church, dad went to check the coal furnace and once again, mother goes upstairs to continue vacuuming the whole of the sanctuary. I was kitchen bound, to clean sinks and counter tops. Then I mopped the kitchen floor and checked for any spills on the cupboards and cleaned them off too. Then I headed to the 30 or so Sunday school rooms to clean the floors and do a general tidy of tables and chairs. *What a family outing!*

The whole bloody day was spent predominately at church. Man!!! Does that make me holy or what? WHY wasn't I a person of worth at this stage of my life? I felt like a "non-entity; a body form going through the appearance of living. WHO had chosen this life-path for me? Was there any significance or real purpose to this life style? WHERE was the justice in the whole overall scheme of things? WHEN would liberty and freedom remove my current chains of bondage? WHAT would my future hold?

The other season I hated was summer. This was the season for a major church cleaning! I was now in grade 11 so I didn't have to go to church after school during the week. But working on the weekends was totally expected! My mother told my father that I should be allowed to get a job after school to start saving for "future education".

On top of that the school work was getting a little more difficult and required more effort on my part to complete assignments. My father begrudgingly accepted this fact, so I was pleased that I was getting a little "free time" away from the church. I would have some time to make money and hopefully partake in a few "after school" activities.

Uh Oh!!! SUMMER... As I have already said, a major cleaning of the entire church would soon be happening. This meant "all hands on deck". Because I was working at a gas station after school, I was able to adjust my hours of work so that I could work at the church during the day and work at the gas station in the late afternoon and evening. I would restock car materials, wash and clean cars, pump gas and do a general "clean-up" that was needed on a daily basis.

Just to remind you... this church was one huge building; 2 storey to boot! Mom and Dad would start on the cleaning and polishing of all the oak pew benches as well as vacuuming the seat cushions. After all, it just wouldn't do for some of these old folks to have to sit on a hard, oak surface. In reality, it may even have kept some of them awake during the sermon.

I would be sent off to the Sunday school rooms which all had vinyl flooring, so I would start to strip the wax surface down. This was done on my hands and knees, with floor stripper and a lot of elbow grease to get down to the bare surface. Once this was done, it was a matter of "re-waxing" the floor and then polish it to a shine. These rooms would not be used again till Fall. Once one room was complete... I just kept moving on until all 30 rooms were finished! As you can imagine, I spent a vast amount of time on my knees in church!

My father and mother worked just as hard as I did and there was no end in sight for any of us. This "beast" required many hours to get it cleaned and polished for the Fall season. There were 3 large banquet halls with hardwood floors in this building that required full attention as well. They too needed to be stripped to the original surface and then re-waxed and polished to a sparkling shine. Thankfully my father had a huge stripper machine to do this task.

Granted this was a heavy machine to move around but at least he didn't have to get on his hands and knees like I did. My mother didn't have it "easy" either, since she had to wash down all the kitchen cupboards inside and out, which required removing all the dishes from the cupboards as well as make sure the dishes were in good condition. She had to note all the dishes that needed to be replaced and keep them separate.

She also vacuumed all the carpeted surfaces; she polished the minister's private office which also had oak walls and had to bring back the luster on that panelling. Then the windows needed to be washed inside and out.

No one got "off the hook" in this job. When I needed a break, I could go outside and cut grass or I could go to the manse... cut and trim the grass and bushes and even wash his car. Guess he felt it would be beneath him to offer to pay a young person to do any of these things for him. However, I always had a feeling that my dad got a little something for doing jobs at the manse; but I never got a nickle extra.

I think that by now, as you read this, you may be getting a small glimpse of my life... or lack of it... and can readily see why "church life" and me are going to become strangers as soon as I can break away from it. I don't ever want to return to this style of "existence".

Before I move away, however, I would be totally amiss if I did not leave a somewhat "hurtful" comment about some of the church parishioners. As I had stated, this church in its time, was quite an impressive building and many of the affluent citizens of the city wanted to be acknowledged as "attending this church" and the "impressive" minister who was affiliated with it.

It was all about "appearances" with some of these folk who I would call "snobs"... just because they were wealthy and each tried to outdo the other in appearance, in the way they moved about and in the donations they gave to the church.

Whenever any one of them would happen to meet me... either at a church function, a banquet or dinner, or a meeting, I was always addressed as "the caretaker's son" and never by my first name, although many knew it but refused to use it.

Many times someone would say... *"Caretaker's son... get me another chair. Clean up that spill."* It was degrading! I always tried to correct them and repeat my first name; but they paid absolutely no attention. They seemed to look at me as if they had just stepped in something unmentionable when they spoke to me. They would often complain to a church elder or would speak to my father about his son being disrespectful to them.

Consequently, my dad would tear a trip off me and I had to hold my tongue in front of my dad. I really was not impressed with the fact that he did this regularly, instead of standing up for me. But then my mother would tell with tears in her eyes... *"Your comments could get your dad fired and then where would this family be? Show them that you are the better person and simply walk away without comment."*

In my wildest dreams, I would never want to hurt my mother, so I really tried to bite my lips and smile at the person's comment. This would really "piss them off"; so I guess I won the occasional round. It gave me a feeling that I had put "the jerk" in his place with a smile and an indifference to what was asked of me.

I always felt I was worthless... just someone who happened to be in this place at this time and time itself seemed endless. I guess in retrospect, the actual winner was the person commenting and asking me to do something they wished done. My single moment of a smile and my indifference, came out in second place. But I had to hang on to that thought that I had felt just a tiny moment of satisfaction, or all would be lost.

I also began to notice that some of these "snobs" would say things and ask things of my mother with their over-bearing tones as well. They seemed it was their "right" to ask and demand her to do their bidding.

How they battered my poor mother and she... like the lady she was... did their "demands" as ordered. I would have like to do otherwise but I was always so impressed about how well my mother took what was handed out. In essence, she was a good mother; always showing me "how" to take it and "how" to be in control of one's emotions; not to let the "idiots" get to you.

My mother had taught me a valuable lesson... not only in this "church" but for living LIFE itself. She taught me how to pick my battles and plan very well for my revenge. My mind would have to work in such a way, that I would be able to get the satisfaction that I needed.

However, forever after, I was never able to have any respect for my father... for his lack of education and for never having any potential drive or "self-worth". I found the man to be strictly an empty shell of a person. I further hated the fact that he dragged both my mother and me into a hard life... all because of *his* short-comings and the fact that he was only concerned about himself and what he could get out of it. He was a very hard man to warm up to and he and I never got close.

My mother was the more "intelligent" of the two and she sensed this lack of emotion between us. Maybe it was because she was able to read my body language or more likely she was very aware of my body actions and read me like a book. She actually took me aside once and said... *"You really don't like your father do you?"* Because I never lied to my mother... not even once... I replied... *"No! Unfortunately I do not like him at all. He is a loser and does not seem to really care about anyone but himself!"*

I saw a tear fall from her eyes and wished I had lied! Seeing those tears really tore me up inside; not because of what I had said. That was the truth; but I had hurt my mother's feelings. God knows that was never my intent... yet again; I learned another lesson in life.

As I told you earlier, I was "allowed" to have a part time job in grades 11 and 12; but full time summer work was never a possibility.

Like most teenagers, I wanted a car; wanted to be able to take a girl out; or just cruise the drag. Most of you might remember that this merely meant to go up and down the Main Street of the city... trying to look "cool" and see if I could get some girls to go for a ride with me and my buddies.

I did find a job at a gas station which would allow me to work right after school for a few hours and also some after-dinner hours until closing time, through the week. I was also able to work Saturdays and Sundays; but had to fit in "church clean-up" times. That was usually finished by noon hour; so going to work at the gas station from 1:00 p.m. until 9:00 p.m. would be available hours for me to have a job.

Finally... I was making money for my labours... not just having a roof over my head and food before me. My father had decided that having these two things were payment enough as my father's "slave". Who ever said life would be "fair" and then you would get your "just rewards"? Obviously it wasn't a church care-taker's son! Believe me!

I had worked a ton of hours at the gas station... every spare moment away from that blasted church work; and my bank account was finally showing some results. It was long overdue and I was feeling some "self-worth" and I took credit for my hard work. I was telling my parents how pleased I was with myself and about the money I had saved.

I was now ready to purchase a car... not a new one by any means; but hopefully one that was not only affordable but basically mechanically fit and had a body worthy of my money. At this point, my father said that he was thinking about getting a newer car and would offer to sell me his "old" car at a "supposedly" fair price.

At this point in my life, I was still a little naive because I thought this could be a logical thing to do. I knew my dad had looked after his car and that the car had not been in any accidents, to have to worry about any frame damage. So, with a stupid smile on my face, I jumped in with both feet; also thinking I would get a "fair price" or even a "family" discount.

Here is where "dear old dad" did the "bugger" deed. He went to the car dealership where he wished to purchase his own car and got a "trade-in-value" they would allow on his transaction. He came home and told me he had found a car he liked and that they were going to offer him "so much" as a trade-in. He decided that he wanted me to pay "that" amount to him for his old car.

I agreed to pay that amount to purchase his car from him because I thought he had been truthful with me. I went with him to the dealership to pick up his new car. I had also seen him put the paperwork in the glove box for safe-keeping. Being curious, I went out to look in "my" glove box to see the paperwork that he had left there.

I was totally SHOCKED! My father got $1,500.00 MORE from me than what the dealership was offering. I was SCREWED by my own greedy father! That takes the cake!! I could have "spit nickles"; but could not approach him on this matter. You see, then I would have to confess that I had sneaked behind his back and looked at his business affairs without permission. I would be calling him a "liar" to his face!

I thought for a long minute... and I am glad I did. I pondered the whole issue and tried to look at it logically and responsibly. Yes, I was hurt – both financially and emotionally – but what stopped me in my tracks was the fact that it would hurt my mother's heart. And "yes" she would cry out about her husband's "meanness" and I did not want to go down that road. I bit my lip and said... *"Someday, old buddy, you and I will either come to blows or I will find a way to get my revenge."*

Yes $1,500 was a financial burden for me; money I should not have had to pay out; but pay it I would, to prevent paining my mother's heart.

About this stage in my life, some goodness was about to befall our family circumstances. My father got a job as a Correctional Officer at the jail. This meant no more working at the church and no more having to "kiss ass" to the members of that church.

In fact, I never wanted to go back to that building again. But My mother requested that I go with her on Mother's Day and at Christmas and we go as a "family". Do I really need to explain "WHO" never went back to that church... ever again?

It was kind of nice to be able to put the "old fogies" in their place when they realized we were no longer "looking after the church". But some of them still had the audacity to ask me to do something for them. I took a special kind of "delight" in being cheeky whenever Mom wasn't too close by. It was kind of satisfying to see the looks on their faces when I refused.

I guess I was truly starting to feel that I was worth something after all. It did my heart good to know that I AM a person of worth.

WHO am I now? A person of worth? WHAT had I accomplished getting the revenge I so desperately wanted? WHY did I finally feel good about myself and the revenge I had gotten? WHEN would the smirk leave my face, so that my mother didn't realize what I had done? WHERE now would this new-found freedom take me?

At this time, my mother also shared that she wanted to fulfil her dream of becoming a nurse. Therefore, she was going to start working in a Doctor's office to see if in fact, this was still on her "bucket list" of things she wanted to accomplish in her lifetime.

At this stage, she was not a "nurse"; but was strictly a Doctor's assistant. She would call people in to see the Doctor; get their charts out for his inspection; assist the elderly into the examining room and be available if the Doctor ever needed her assistance. My mother was always a "people" person; very pleasant and always polite and helpful.

When she came home, she would discuss her day with us at the supper table... never mentioning any names; but strictly talked about the circumstances and she seemed to thoroughly enjoy this new experience. If we were lucky, my father, who worked shift work would either be at work, or sleeping before his next shift.

However, he also could be at the table as well. But talk about Mister "gloom and doom". His very presence in my life was not a welcome sight; but one that I had to tolerate. Fortunately, his presence at the supper table was not a regular occurrence.

I was now totally allowed to work as much as I wanted at the gas station... after school; after dinner; on weekends... even through the summer if I chose. I had been working quite a while for my boss and he was always happy that I was so readily available. He was even enjoying a little more leisure time and knew that I was a pretty responsible and reliable employee. I could assist with a lot of the jobs at hand since I had some experience and was trustworthy.

I had been burning the candle at both ends... so to speak... for a long time now. Previously, I had been working at the church, at the gas station, fitting in homework and assignments... and it was starting to burn me out. However, I was still just able to get a passing school mark; but then a new "situation" was about to enter my life.

In our High School, there was a thing called the "Honour Society". It was for those students who were able to get high marks and they were rewarded with "red blazers" to help "set them off" from the rest of the student body. These students had an air of "arrogance" about them and would "strut" around like peacocks in their pretty red jackets, pretending to be "better than everyone else".

Can you see what's coming next? There happened to be several of them; so it was likely there would be one in my class... pretty good odds. There was one girl... an honour student... who was a real "piece of work". She thought that she was *special* and I felt it was my job to "break her bubble".

Because I now had a new sense of "freedom" I told her that *"anyone could have honour marks if they choose to do so; but most of us did not like the dumb red blazers and the society as a whole."*

Not only did I open my big mouth; but put both feet in it as well! The challenge was on! She thought nothing like this would EVER happen in a million years. So we made a bet; and for the life of me, I don't remember what it was. But I knew she was NOT going to get the upper hand and I would be totally applying myself to put her "out of the game".

Now I did not have the luxury of study time; or of putting extra efforts into the subject matter at hand. Remember, I worked 2 jobs plus school. So time never permitted extra time and effort. To my knowledge, all the honour society members had parents with good jobs, so working and going to school was not an option for them. All they had to do was go to school and enjoy a leisurely life style.

Naturally, this was good for them; but they did not realize the "real" world was where most of us had to work and also go to school. It was a totally different life style and I would think that this could cramp their life-style and their "honour" marks in the school system.

I knew who I was and where I was going and why I was going in the direction I was. It was also apparent that a "mission" had been laid at my feet and for the first time in the school system, I was prepared, willing and able to go after this "gold ring" of achievement; not only to prove to myself, but also to put "that girl" in her place. It would indeed make my life rich and full to remove the "smug look" from her face and to walk across the stage... either in front of or behind her... to receive my *honour pin.* It would be receiving the greatest satisfaction of my time in High School and would also validate that I **was** capable of being an "honour student".

I guess the sad thing would be that because I was in grade 12 and it was my final year, there would be no red blazer for me. But it would also show that I had been there; done that; and had shown myself worthy of the honour society. It would also be more important to witness my mother's tears of overwhelming joy as I completed a task that I was told "I could not do" and in the end, I had come out a *WINNER!*.

WHO I was and my capabilities had now been proven. WHAT I was capable of doing when I set my mind to the task at hand, I had proven to myself. WHAT was the drive within me to prove, given the same level playing field to all, that anyone could display their very best? WHEN was proving to myself that my *word was my bond in attaining my goals*, so important to me? WHERE was proving to myself that my future was positive and not being put down... was important to show others?

I would be amiss if I did not point out a certain "circumstance" that was an obstacle that I would have to overcome in order to have gotten that "honour pin". I was in the 4-year business course, which meant that certain subjects were mandatory in order to have a full credit for the school year. One of the subjects introduced was typing and shorthand in grade 11. In grade 12, we polished our skill level to better prepare us for the working world and for the expectations of a business/commercial graduate.

Herein lay the task at hand and the obstacle that I had to overcome to succeed. In grade 11, I had a teacher who was "an old maid" (unmarried) and one who did NOT like boys/men... even in her wildest imagination. A business course was not typical for most males attending high school; but rather it was more normal for boys to go into the "trade" courses... mechanics, electrical, plumbers, carpenters etc. The few of us who went into the commercial course were really the "odd balls" in the system.

This particular teacher made it quite plain that she was NOT impressed that we were in her class. To this extent, she would completely ignore us as much as possible. She would always address the class with words like... *"How are my girls today?"* Then she would proceed to lay out the assignment for that day's class.

In this class of typing, there was always part of the class routine to have a "typing test", to see who would be the better student in that particular class. At the end of the test she would say... *"Which one of my girls had typed "this speed" or "that speed"?"* Then she would examine the test results and pass out a card in recognition of that particular speed.

It didn't matter if any one of the few guys in the class had their hand up; she would always try to overlook them and strictly go to the girls who had their hands up. I had a gut feeling that she was only out to give the guys a "passing grade" and that was her total intention. I knew that because I was in a contest with the honour student to get an "honour pin" myself, I would have to be recognized in her class in order to obtain a higher mark than what she had in mind.

I would wave my hand over my head in an attempt to be recognized; but that usually did not work out too well. My next approach was to call out her name in class, but with a "twist". She always made a point of correcting you if you called her "Mrs." instead of "Miss". Consequently, that was what I did. I called her "Mrs." to annoy her to the point that she would come down to my station to correct me and give me a "tongue lashing" for doing this. I worked very hard to get my speed up as well as my accuracy, in order to get a higher grade mark. So this was the "mission at hand".

This school term was in the 1960's... *the "cave days"* to today's standards. So the typewriters were "old" Underwood manual machines. It was not until grade 12 that the electric machine came into the school system. I want to lay the ground work so that you will better appreciate the humour of this typing class experience. When the electric typewriters arrived in grade 12, the old "MONARCH" only gave that typewriter to the girls and left the 3 guys in the class with the old manual machines.

Now the test period game was on! I was not going to let this "old lady" have the upper hand in this game. I typed my heart out and as I looked at my typing test when it was completed, I waited for the "old gal's" voice. *"Which one of my girls has this type of score?"* Several hands went up... along with mine. Then she said... *"Which one of my girls thinks she has a little higher score than that?"* A few less hands went up this time, as well as mine. This seemed to take forever and my hand kept going up at every score level. I could see she noticed my hand going up every time.

I could sense her disdain that perhaps I had beaten one of her "girls". Finally with the continued waving of my hand and my single comment of "Mrs." she was down at my desk in a shot. *"Just what do you think you have accomplished... as if you could even come close to an electric machine?"* I told her that I had a speed of fifty (50) words per minute with a 99.6% accuracy, which none of her girls was even close to that mark.

She peeled the piece of typing paper out of my machine so fast it left the rollers spinning and she made her way back to her desk in an attempt to discredit me in front of the whole class. The look on her face told me I was looking forward to a total embarrassment in front of everyone. She also thought that I had such nerve to even think I was in that kind of league.

Usually the dear old girl would get one of her girls with the high mark to stand up and have the class applaud her for her abilities, while she handed out a certificate of accomplishment. Well, she <u>finally</u> came back to my desk, after scrutinizing the page every possible way... up, down, sideways... trying to find an error.

She had such a disgusting look on her face as she marched down to my desk; flung my certificate of accomplishment on the desk and turned around... muttering under her breath all the way to her own desk. There was no recognition from the class and certainly no applause for a job well done. She simply told the class to go on to the next assignment, as she did a slow boil at her desk.

<u>WHO</u> did she think she was and why had she this much power to control? <u>WHAT</u> had made her so bitter and crotchety in her old age, that she seemed so miserable? <u>WHERE</u> did she think her attitude would take her in the teaching profession? <u>WHEN</u> would she cut some slack in her thinking and try to treat everyone in her class with equality? <u>WHY</u> did she have this nasty attitude toward males? <u>WHAT</u> painful memories haunted her?

Well, it didn't matter to me that I didn't get any class "recognition". I knew I had done well and had proven to myself that I could do it! Life was rich and full!

I continued to excel at typing, always beating the highest score of any of the girls in class. Since I was of no importance to the teacher, she never acknowledged my success. She never again examined one of my typing pages; but she did acknowledge my excellence in the exam.

The same results were experienced in the shorthand course because I was always able to take down the dictation and transcribe the results... often more quickly than the female students. Unfortunately, the teacher always had a very stern look on her face and never acknowledged the fact that "I" was so good at this job as well. I guess, in retrospect, her losing to a male, was a hard pill to swallow.

She effectively put a wall between us; but she did record the marks and no one outside the class was any wiser.

She retired at the end of that school term. I know I had shaken her world and suspect she could no longer take another year like this. Although more than likely, she was at the"retirement" age and decided to leave teaching. I also suspect that "I" was the victor and I had "gotten to her" and I was satisfied!

WHY was it so important to feel that I got revenge? WHAT difference did it make in my life? WHEN would I ever get over having to "get even" with someone who offended me? WHERE was this feeling of "revenge" coming from? WHO would finally "wake me up" to the fact that revenge was NOT necessary?

So ended my High School years... 4 years had passed and it had not even registered. I was still not totally aware of who I was; where I was going in life; and what lay before me. I was at my wit's end and my brain was shutting down. It was like my life was at a stand-still.

It was the same kind of feeling I had as a child. People did things for me; told me where to go; what to do and when to do it. My very existence now depended on **my** taking control of my own destiny. Naturally I was scared that I would screw up and that the important people in my life would not respect me or my decisions.

For the moment, the course of action was clear. Go back to the gas station for the summer. Maybe enough time would be available to plot my next course of action.

My dear mother was still very much active in her church. Not me! But I went with my mother on Mothers' Day and at Christmas as I had promised. As fate would have it, my mother knew several people and their various occupations. While talking to one of the other members, she discovered that he taught at a community college and was very keen on the courses that were being offered, as well as the potential for getting a good job at completion.

I guess, in hind site, I had done the right thing about getting a summer job and letting "fate" take me by the hand in its infinite wisdom. My life seemed to be bent on some kind of career or occupation; so I let things happen as fate wished.

Thank God for my mother's actions because I still had no idea at this point about what I was going to do. I did not have enough money to go to university; although I suspect I did have the academic marks that were good enough. I knew I didn't want to work at the gas station for the rest of my life and the jobs my buddies got in factories did not impress me either.

So it was with a light heart that I accepted my new "fate"... thanks to my mother and her contacts in the field of education. At this point in my life, I realized that I was still not a person of "great worth". I suspected "that kind of person" would know exactly what they wanted out of life. For too long, I had let those around me "set my direction in life" and I was being blown along by the wind in whatever direction seemed to be selected for me.

I was putting one foot in front of the other... not really in control... and certainly not being aware of being able to stand on my own two feet. Consequently I did not consider myself "a man"... merely a robot in motion. But the day soon arrived when college life was to begin... new surroundings, new rules, new students, new routine.

I felt like a sheep being led to slaughter so I went into my shell of "security" and allowed myself to follow the pack and not create any waves. No one seemed to notice my existence and I certainly had no desire to stand out in the crowd. I was always a shy lad and so my shell of existence was indeed my "security blanket" as college life began.

Here too, I allowed others to take charge and when I arrived in my first classroom, I calmly and quietly took a back seat. Hopefully I would not be noticed by fellow students or by the instructor. This system seemed to work out positively for me as fellow students went about getting actively involved in class and in the life of the college.

Guess I was just the "student" who would be his own worst enemy. I kept to myself; did my assignments; studied hard and long; and so when exam time came around, I did very well on them. I was totally involved in the subject at hand and my marks proved I was excelling at the subjects.

However, this soon back-fired on me! The instructor would call out my name and sing praises about my marks. *Oh God!* I became the centre of attention... certainly NOT where I wanted to be. *Why couldn't he simply record the marks and let the whole issue die?* Every student in the class swung around and looked straight at me! Comments like... *"nerd; bookworm; get a life"* came back at me! This was certainly not my intention in the farthest reaches of my mind; it was totally opposite of what I wanted! I did NOT want to stand out in any way, shape or form!

I guess to some extent, I had been a "bookworm". No one wanted to bother with me anyway and I had wanted to be "on my own". I was so shy and even that didn't seem normal to me. What was wrong with me? How does one overcome this shyness? How do I become a normally noticed person whom people would like to talk to and to spend time with?

Obviously I was lacking big time, in the social skills of life. It was something I was always going to be pursuing; but like the gold ring of success, it was always just outside my reach and would forever be my quest in life.

With the completion of the first college course, summer vacation time was upon me and that meant "summer employment" to pay the cost for next year's course. I was fortunate in this endeavour because it was "guaranteed" with the course I was taking. It would give students the practical side of the course in preparation for the second term.

CHANGE was one word I really disliked. My summer employment was to be in the northernmost part of the province and so another adjustment to my living style, my location and my daily routine was in line. My "comfort zone" was now gone and I was feeling adrift.

This placement was a 4-month exile from home. There would be new living conditions, new people, new job and a new life-style. Would I be up to the task? I nervously took on this endeavour with mixed feelings and was really hoping for the best! Granted, I knew it was only four months and I knew I would be paid. This was extremely positive as far as I was concerned.

Once I got to my destination and settled in, things didn't seem too bad. I thought I could handle it. Self-doubt is a terrible thing; but once the routine of job settled in, I just knew I could handle it. And handle it I did!

Before I realized it I was back home and had a few days to re-adjust before heading back to college life. I promised myself that I would try harder to mix with people and be a little more "out-going". Oh, I know... "talk is cheap"... and soon I was back in my own "secluded world" of hitting the books; studying like a trooper. It seemed that I had not gained any self-confidence at all over the last 4 months.

WHY was I so lacking in self-confidence? Did I get that from my father who didn't have any in his life time and didn't even seem to like people at all? WHAT, if anything was the true significance of me being so introverted? WHEN... if ever... would I come out of my "shell" or "bubble" of existence? WHO was I really? Why could I not discover my true identity? WHERE was this "person of worth" hiding? Why was I always hiding in the shadows of my secure world?

Once again, I did very well on the course and my marks were excellent; to the point that I was asked to join a company without the hassle of any job interviews. Granted, it was a minor job with a new company but I Knew at the time that the job was mine and this interview was just a "formality".

I was pleased with myself. In fact I actually thought that I did well in the interview and hoped that it would be enough to help kick-start my confidence! I now was fully employed and the world now lay before me... to explore and to start to build a life for myself and settle into life with a life-long, loving partner and the warmth of a home environment.

For most people this would be the "norm"; but for me, I felt it would never be obtained because of my shyness and my lack of social skills and confidence with the opposite sex. It all seemed such a huge wall to try and climb and too big an obstacle to overcome. I was still alone, shy, afraid to make contact. I was never comfortable around the ladies; so I had to push myself even to have a conversation. Asking a girl out on a date seemed like a dream and nowhere near reality for me.

After many years of being on my own, a new female secretary came into the office on a short-term replacement for a gal who was on maternity leave. I started to hang around her desk whenever I was able to attempt to build up enough confidence to ask her out. The more time I spent talking with her, the more comfortable I was feeling. I finally got up my courage and asked her out on a date... and she accepted!

WHO was the person in this body that finally stepped up to the plate... with new-found courage? WHAT made me feel that I needed to bring gifts on our first outing? Was it good manners or an attempt to "buy" the date? WHEN was this acceptable on the first date or was this to be the "norm"? I was out of my element with experience in this. WHY did I feel so nervous and so unsure of myself and my self-worth? <u>WHERE</u> in my thinking process was I going to be able to figure out this dating process?

I was on pins and needles as I arrived at her townhouse to go for our dinner date. I brought her a dozen yellow roses and a bottle of wine; guess I was hoping to make a good impression. Obviously I did the right thing because I was greeting with a smile and a kiss to thank me. *So far... so good!*

We went to a "classy" restaurant and I hoped that a further date might be in store for us. The conversation went well as we both started to open up about our lives... both past and present and we were both getting comfortable with one another.

I discovered she was a single parent with 2 kids to support and a very absent "ex-husband" so there was certainly no money coming from him and her life was difficult. *A red flag went up!* If I was smarter and listened to my "gut instinct" I would have run... not walked away from this situation. But I was thoroughly enjoying myself; the meal and the conversation and this was my first date as a mature young man and my confidence was growing.

Since she did not know how long to book the babysitter, she had to get home fairly quickly after dinner. Yes, I was a "rookie" at this dinner thing and didn't know how to plan anything further, so I took her home. As we walked to her doorway there was an awkward moment. Do I kiss her goodnight? She thanked me again for the roses and the dinner.

To my surprise and amazement, she made the first move for a good night kiss. She took charge and we enjoyed a long, passionate kiss. As I turned to leave, she asked if I was in a hurry.

There was a bottle of wine still to drink. I thought... *"Hey; the evening is still young."* I felt like the fly being invited into the spider web. She could tell I was totally inexperienced in the "dating game" and could probably have some fun and adventure with this "Poor, naïve, and dumb creature. She thought she might reap some benefits from this "poor, naive, dumb creature". Again, my gut was reacting to this new stress level and was feeling very uncomfortable. Should I run? Should I just get out of here while I can?

<u>WHY</u> was I not listening to the logic of my brain? <u>WHAT</u> dream world was I trying to live in? <u>WHEN</u> would I realize what was happening? <u>WHERE</u> were my expectations leading? <u>WHO</u> would awaken me?

As I walked into the house, I really did not understand what I was doing here. Why was I totally unaware of what was happening? I was not comfortable at all but my legs would not allow me to walk to the door and leave! I knew I was going to be very sorry shortly... both mentally and financially.

As Barnum and Bailey once stated... *A sucker is born every minute!...* Guess who is the newest member of this "club"? Even with my eyes wide open, I walked right in to the whole "complex"... unwed mother and the whole family, living in a subsidized housing unit. Obviously, my brain was not functioning as it should have, and I would be the worst off from this endeavour.

Again, I have to ask **who** is this person in my body and **what** in the world was I thinking? Oh yes... I was NOT thinking at all about **what** was "life". How in the world was I allowing myself to be in this situation? **Why** was I allowing myself to be a "worthless" person?

As I had said... this was my first *real* adult date with a woman who seemingly wanted to be in my life and this new feeling of "self-worth" was totally refreshing. I wanted it to continue. All the red flags that were going up were totally unseen by me... whether I willingly put them out of sight or chose not to recognize them at all.

I was a fool and would not; nor could not acknowledge that fact! This lady possessed a lot more life skills than what I had. Like a master chess player, she knew where to place the chess tools to win the game off this novice player. She moved the chess tools with skill... just enough to intrigue me; but not enough to scare me away.

Again, **why** was I allowing her to take charge of my life? Was I so starved for love and affection and a feeling of self-worth? I liked the idea of being able to be a "member of society" and have a lady in my life. At this point however, she kept the children out of the "relationship".

In my little "bubble of reality" I was going through the motions of a "normal" relationship of regularly talking on the phone, making plans for the weekend, feeling like someone thought enough of me to have me in their life. I could not even imagine the "horrors" that were in store for me. I was totally consumed with this lady and showering her with affection and gifts. I think at this moment, I was totally **brain dead**.

She became creative like an artist, creating a fine piece of work, to the point where she felt she could now put forth some "demands"... what she "expected" from me in return, for me remaining in her life. I had become "too comfortable" with what she had created and I was enjoying being "king of the castle".

She suggested quite strongly that I should buy her a house and she would pay rent to live there. She did not want her children living in this subsidized housing unit and I agreed that the conditions did leave a lot to be desired. The next big change was the introduction of her children.

I was now to be in their presence on a "regular" basis... family dinners, watching TV together, or just having them about. Until this time, she had kept them away from me at all costs. *Oh boy!!!! Wake up!* In all honesty, I was not enjoying having children in my world at all.

They were constantly making demands on their mother or just being "pests". This may seem "normal" to an ordinary family; but to an outsider, it was very annoying and I told their mother that. Like any mother, she went on the defensive and I was "put in my place" very quickly. In my defence, I did not have "the balls" to say *enough is enough* and end the relationship.

Again, I asked myself **why** am I here, in this place? **Why** was I so starved for affection that I was allowing myself to be subjected to this kind of stress? **Why** did I have no backbone, willing to accept whatever was being handed out?

As I have repeatedly said, I was very shy and found it extremely difficult to form bonds of friendship. It has always been hard for me to talk to women... particularly if I were asking for a date or even a friendly conversation. I existed "in the background"; never wanting to stand out. I didn't understand why I was like that! Was I like my father and had no self-confidence? Was this to be my "fate"... being a "nobody"?

Maybe I have answered my own question about why I was a "willing fool"... longing for someone to love me; to be recognized as a person of worth. Maybe it was simply that I was sad and unhappy and was willing to do whatever it took to feel "alive". I guess I have always been my own "worst enemy" and have come to "accept" that I was a nobody and whatever fate was to be my destiny was "okay". This sounds pretty sad! But it was who I was and I would remain in this existence for a good part of my life!

Now my new life was beginning to take new form, like the structure of a new building. The hole had been dug, the basement foundation poured, and the structure framing was now underway. Like a foreman on a construction site, she observed the whole building procedure to its completion. The home now was completed. She and her children were ready to move in as her architectural plans had been fulfilled. Life was again a "bowl of cherries" as the saying goes... "if mother is not happy; no-one is happy". This faze of our life together had been completed; so now she was happy.

<u>WHY</u> had I let my self-respect be driven out of my brain? <u>WHAT</u> had happened to my self-worth? <u>WHO</u> was now controlling my every action? <u>WHEN</u> would I have the strength of conviction to break these emotional chains that bound me now? <u>WHERE</u> is my destiny to be happy? Where did it go?

I would spend weekends living in "her" house and for a time that was acceptable. No further demands were being made... **yet**. I guess that because I was living there on the weekends, that no rent was required. Like the dummy I was becoming, I didn't want to make any waves; so I went along with this situation till she wanted something else.

There was to be another change on my horizon from the life style I was currently living. I was totally caught off guard by what was to be an ever life changing occurrence. This was to be one in hind sight that had I a backbone I would not have agreed to.

The next item up for discussion was marriage. She had been keeping the children on a low profile during my weekend stays and had even become more affectionate towards me, which had not been the previous normal demeanour on her part. I was enjoying once again the feeling of happiness and even to the point of regaining my self-worth. I should have realized that this was leading me to a big mistake on my part, but still the conversation continued.

She had once again, like the master Chess player she was, moved me along in this game of life. She moved her Chess tools slowly destroying mine in the process, to accomplish yet another winning game. I thought she was sincere and wonderful and that her desire was for us to be a couple and build a life together. *What a fool I was to believe this fairy-tale!!* Indeed, the marriage was put in motion and with me having the money, and she having the plans for the marriage, the contract was completed... and I was out a lot of money.

Once we were married, her last name became mine. Now in according with the laws of the land she would receive half of our joint possessions, if/when the marriage ended.

She was learned student after her first marriage had ended. She did not want to end up with the same disastrous results as with the first marriage. She was now playing her cards close to her chest so that she would come out the winner in the end.

She still was not satisfied with her current living conditions. She wanted a much larger home to be the "so-called" family home. It was time once again to get out the Chess board game, as unbeknownst to me; she had been scouting a new larger home in the country as her new accusation.

Once again, like a master Chess player, she skillfully, accurately and slowly moved the Chess tools to win yet another game. Again, being a novice Chess player, I provided very little competition, as not knowing the game and the significance of the value of each tool, it was really a one sided game.

Because I gave into her, I was back in this "mystical" place where I was the centre of attention. Again, I believed that everything was all right in my world. Again, I fell under her spell. I was just a poor, dumb naive fool.

I have no doubt that you can see where all this is going! I was just merrily going along for the ride and totally unaware of the fate that was to await me. WHY was I so naive? WHY was I so unaware of my fate? WHY was I unable to see the larger picture? Why was I allowing myself to be put into this situation? WHERE was my backbone? WHY was I such a fool?

Was I so in need of someone to love me and let me feel that I had a "soul-mate", that I could not see the forest for the trees? They say hind-sight makes everything clear; but I was totally consumed and was being played like an insignificant tool in a Chess game... doing and going where I was told and doing everything that was being asked of me in this nursery tale of a "life style".

The first piece of the puzzle was being put into place with the purchase of the home "she" wanted and life was very pleasant for me. No waves were being created and it seemed smooth sailing. Soon I would see the next "quest" of the day. We could not have a "new" home with "old furniture". Consequently, she would like new furniture to take with her. Out comes my wallet again and in reality, the new furniture for the house was purchased.

Now... here comes the last piece of the puzzle. She needed a car! After all, since this new house was in the country, she needed a mode of transportation. As she said very clearly... *"I can't always be waiting on you and your time table!"* So the deed was done and the car was purchased to her satisfaction.

Harmony was still part of my world; although my bank account was almost non-existent. Like the owner of the Barnum & Bailey circus stated... *"A sucker is born every minute!"* May I introduce myself as the "newest" sucker?

Where was my head at? **When** was I going to come out of this bubble of make-believe? **Why** was I so out of touch with reality? **What** was I waiting for? The hammer was looming over my head and why was I not getting out of the way? **Who** did I think would save me? I could not see the "big picture" to the total restructuring of this family unit. Life at the moment to me seemed in total harmony. I could not see in my wildest imagination the under lying force at work. It was ever so slowly moving forward not creating any waves or suspicion whatsoever. She wanted to improve the finances of this home by finding another job... a better-paying job; one where she could help with the household expenses. Somehow I thought she might be sincere in her wishes to help with expenses to create a better way of life for all of us.

I am quite sure you all know what *"Out of sight; out of mind"* means. Now we were working at different locations; with different hours of employment. If she wanted to do things on her own, who would be the wiser? Certainly not me! I was not even remotely in her league because I was playing an *"honest"* game.

It was at this point that I could finally see that she was beginning to change... become more distant; less caring. She was creating a totally new life for herself and her children.

Slowly, my life was becoming a "hell", living under the same roof and we were now like total strangers. She did not want me participating in whatever was happening in her world; nor was she interested in anything that was happening in my world. Life was very bleak to the point of me becoming depressed; but she took absolutely no notice of me at all.

WHAT had I done wrong in this relationship? WHY should I now be getting the shaft? WHEN should my brain have kicked into gear to help me? WHERE was my destiny in life... my life that was about to come crashing down upon my head? WHO is to blame? The fault is mine... totally mine. I wanted true love (a soul mate); faith in a fellow human being. All this was now just a faint memory.

I totally knew at this point that all was lost. The marriage was now a thing of the past. It was after some consideration that both parties felt it was time to put those wheels into motion. According to the law of the land she would receive money from the sale of the house. She would also be entitled to a portion of the house furnishing. This would allow her to set up her new life in the road of her "exploration". Yes, she even had a car for her transportation needs. I had mine and this one I bought so she could get to work once I had bought the home in the country. All in all this was a short "Merry go round" of married life as only a year and a half had passed. Now she was ready to see where her future would take her.

I try not to be too critical of this woman; but there is a "Dutch saying" which puts it into perspective for me... *"Too soon old; too late smart".* Yes, I was totally taken in by this woman. She had played her Chess game very well... and I apparently had just learned some new life skills. It was both mentally and financially a very costly lesson to have learned... but it had indeed cut to my very bone of existence. I guess as the saying goes... "It cost money to play the game, so do not play if you are not prepared to loose".

I didn't even use "common sense" in this relationship. I let every painful blow strike me squarely in the face and in the heart! How could I have become this person of "no worth"?

I had a veil of stupidity over my face; lacking any kind of intelligence to even recognize that life cannot always be taken with a grain of salt; that there is (or should be) a reaction to one's actions. **Where** am I headed now? **What** should I do? **How** do I handle this pain? **Why** am I here in this body? *Is there a shop where I can turn this body in and get a new and "improved" body and spirit to continue on in this wheel of life?*

At this point, I must give credit where credit is due. A mother's love is within each of us all throughout our lifetime. In my heart of hearts, I believe this is why God gave us such a wonderful gift... *not only at birth; but all through our lifetime.* Mother is a constant, always available, always a shoulder to cry on, always willing to help out in whatever capacity. In the animal world, a mother taught her newborn the skills needed to survive and then she leaves them. But a Mother is like a solid rock... a strong foundation to support you throughout your life and to be there during all the ups and downs that may come your way. *Thank God for our Mothers!*

My mother knew. She did what I most needed at that particular time. She gave me a hug! She also gave me a shoulder to cry on and comforted my spirit that was so wounded during this stressful time in my life. She helped put things into perspective, never judging me for my faults. I probably have very many; but she did show there was light at the end of the tunnel. However, it was going to be a very hard road to walk; but she did not say it was *"impossible"*. On the other hand, my father was not the least bit concerned about his son and his broken heart. It didn't affect him personally; so *he didn't even care!*

To him I was totally unimportant! He offered no money to help me; no shoulder to comfort me and absolutely no emotional support. To him I was a *"non-entity"*; a *"nothing of any importance"*. He was my father... in name only! He had been around me during my growing up; but was basically *"done with me"*. Since he could no longer use my time for his own benefit, he had no use for me at all.

So it was, that my mother took me under her wing; she gave me confidence, understanding and total support. In fact she gave me everything I desperately needed. Let me share a little of my mother's wisdom. She told me she had read a valuable message from a book some time ago and the message had stayed in her heart from that point onwards.

"Laugh when you can; apologize when you should and let go of what you cannot change." Life's too short to be anything BUT happy!" Only a mother's love for her child's well-being could come up with the appropriate words to help heal her son's broken heart and spirit.

She told me she didn't want to see me lose the house investment and all the money I had put into it from the time I bought it. So she came up with her own plan! She approached my soon-to-be ex-wife and asked her how much money she would take to walk away. My mother was a wise woman and she told this woman that *"you and my son"* had not put much equity into the home so far. What cash figure would she take to simply walk away?

Both parties knew it would take a while to sell the house; plus pay the real estate agent and the lawyer... that any money she was "expecting" would take a long time to be realized. My mother appealed to her sense of urgency and because she could be able to put her hands on a lot of cash in a hurry, she could simply *"walk away"* and enjoy a new life.

THIS WORKED! The money figure was agreed upon; payment made; a date for her departure was mentioned. It was a hard, bitter pill to swallow. On my arrival home from work one day I found the vast majority of the house contents GONE... even down to a lot of dishes and pots and pans that she thought she should have! Needless to say I was a little shocked because the move-out date she had mentioned to me was totally different. I guess she wanted the *last laugh* at my expense!

In a way I was lucky too, because I did not have to bear seeing all the "stuff" I had purchased being moved and fighting to keep the things I thought I should have. Thus, *her* life was rich and full again. She was the winner **again**.

To make things better for me, I no longer had to bear another night with the stress and tension that was the constant atmosphere in the house. Hopefully you can see the "positive side" of this picture. But the pain, the hurt and the disappointment in my life's choice was very much evident every time I looked in the mirror. WHY was I such an idiot? WHY did I have this invisible "S" on my forehead for all to see? WHY was I not a person of worth? WHEN would I realize all my faults and try to curb them?

They say that life goes on; but does one really want life to go on after all this pain? How long before the pain leaves my body and my soul is at peace? How long before the stress, the anxiety, trying to put one foot in front of the other, trying to carry on in this life amid all the misery that is at my door is at an end? **Do** I at this point in life, really want to be here? **Who** is this person in this body who can never seem to find happiness?

I realized that I had many commitments to fulfil at the bank and to my mother... even to myself to try and be a new and improved version of what was currently "me". I was not ready for "society" at this point. Consequently, merely going to work, coming home to a now empty house, trying to keep my spirits up... was about all that I could manage in my current situation. So it was to be a long, hard road of return to the world that I had left behind. I became a *"modern-day"* hermit, staying within my *"self-made"* world of security. I was not involved in outside activities or people. Thank goodness I was living in the country and there were not many people around to have to try and explain my life-style to anyone.

As if I hadn't had enough zingers thrown in my direction, the mortgage on the house was up for renewal soon. Surprise! My mortgage rate was going from 10.25% to 18.75%. It felt like another nail was being driven into my "coffin".

Even with me tightening my belt, there was no money left in my budget to buy food. All my money went to pay the house bills and the bank mortgage! Once again... thank God for my mother! She would either buy me groceries or have me at her home for dinner. *Dear old dad* was not always too happy to see me there.

But my mother said very clearly... *"The boy is trying his best to make ends meet and I do all the food preparation! What's the big problem?"* He would simply make a face and then go back to reading the newspaper... a good way to block me from having to look at me. Believe me, it was a very long three years of a high mortgage rate and it did top at 22.5% at its highest. Once locked into a mortgage, the Trust Company would **NOT** allow me to get out of any payments.

My mother was constantly worried about my state of mind. She even asked me once if I was "suicidal". I reassured her that I was not quite there yet. Then quickly had to say that I was "making a joke". It would take me 12 years to get through this phase of my life... or my "non-existence". I was totally depressed and merely stumbling along in life; totally emotionless. I felt I had no real quality of life and no one... *except my mother*... who even cared that I was alive!

<u>WHY</u> was I here in this seemingly hellish world? <u>WHAT</u> had my purpose being in life... if anything to help someone else to get ahead in her own world. <u>WHEN</u> was it going to be "my turn" for a little love, a little happiness, someone to care about me? <u>WHERE</u> does this journey begin or end? Was my life only meant to stay in an "up and down" state for ever? <u>WHO</u> other than my mother actually cared if I was alive or dead?

I had dated a girl before my "marriage" and we seemed to have just slipped away from one another. Life has a way of doing that, unless you are actively searching or trying to stay in touch with someone. Hence, this girl had moved on in her life and in my mistake of a marriage I had moved on as well. However, we had a chance encounter at a gas station.

Each of us was there for fuel at the same time and we both said that it must have been "fate" that brought us there at the same time. We decided that since she had some free time and since I had all the time in the world, to have a quick coffee break and chat about "old times".

Maybe we could pick up where we had left off? We seemed to "click" and the conversation did flow quite readily from both of us. I am sure the "prescribed" 10 minutes time was not honoured; but probably it was about 3 times that long we enjoyed time together. We discovered that neither of us had a "significant other"... that we should make plans either to go to a show or have a dinner date to see where things might take us. We still wanted to chat so we decided to go to dinner.

I could not believe what had just happened to me. Was I dreaming? Was life actually going to hand me a *"bowl of cherries"* instead of the usual *"bowl of pits"*? I was both pleased and shocked at the same time. Did I dare think positive thoughts? Was this a sign of "good" coming my way? I quickly got hold of myself. I said... *"Steady old man. Let's not put the cart before the horse. Slow and easy is the way to go. Don't put a lot of hope and expectations on this one dinner. Come down to earth. There is no magic bubble."*
Going too fast was wrong for a couple of reasons. The lady might be scared away before anything can begin or I might make a lot of mistakes in my actions toward her. None the less, slow and easy was the right approach at this early stage. Maybe it was simply a chance encounter after all.

WHAT was now happening in my life? WHERE did this new life experience actually come from? WHO was this person in this body that was so ready to jump from the frying pan into the fire? WHEN will my brain cells kick in and tell me this venture is "right" or "wrong" for me. WHY is this happening now and why is my heart... NOT my brain running my body?

A moment of clarity came to mind, as I thought it might be better to walk *alone in life*... if that were to be my fate. I did NOT want to walk into another bad relationship! Too bad I didn't take this wisdom to heart.

But my heart was longing for a connection to someone so it blocked my brain's ability to apply logic and common sense to what I was about to do. Yet again would I be deeply hurt and end up with a second broken heart?

WHEN would I ever learn? WHO allows himself to seek out pain and unhappiness with ease?

<u>WHY</u> was my life so difficult when it came to matters of the heart? <u>HOW</u> could I never see the light at the end of the tunnel of mistakes? <u>WHO</u> was this person anyway? <u>WHY</u> was I so unable to use the brains God gave me to think about actions and re-actions in my life? <u>WHERE</u> would I find the end of "despair" and get off this merry-go-round of unhappiness? <u>WHAT</u> would it take to end these bad decisions that I seem to be constantly making?

I was now at a crossroads of making a decision about a new relationship. Should I just walk away before I get hurt again? Should I have learned from my past mistakes? Should I try harder to be all that I can be in this new relationship?

My heart won out over my brain! The dinner date would move forward as planned. The evening was a total surprise and delightful. I was starting to question my doubts. The meal and the evening seemed like a dream... almost perfect. I was totally happy for the first time in a long while and I enjoyed this new and strange feeling. It seemed as if my bad luck streak had finally ended and a positive path lay before me.

We made plans to see each other again. We were going to a show and then out for drinks. I could hardly wait for the weekend but it seemed it was going to have a "twist". She brought along her girlfriend/roommate as a "threesome". But she explained that her girlfriend was feeling depressed and needed an evening out. So I simply smiled and agreed this was not a problem; but in reality, I was very displeased.

I was seated next to the girlfriend for the whole evening. Should not red flags be going up all over the place? But I chose not to say anything and had no idea what my next plan of action was going to be.

I was invited for a barbeque and drinks the next weekend. I let myself foolishly believe that it would be just the two of us! Boy what a fool I was! There were several people there and they had all been drinking for some time. When I arrived I was introduced to everyone; but getting drunk apparently was the order of the day.

WHY had I not heeded the red flags that were constantly going up? WHO was this new lady friend and why was a party life-style the order of the day? WHAT was I about to get into? WHEN would I come to my senses and realize this was not "my" life-style? WHERE was the opening to excuse myself and leave?

I knew at this point I had to make a decision about whether to stay or just make an excuse and leave. I decided to stay because the food smelled so good and being alone was not something I wanted. I was totally blown away with the quantity of alcohol that was being consumed and so I made a point of helping to serve drinks. Consequently nobody noticed that I was not drinking.

Even with all the drinking, the food was very tasty and I had gotten away with just drinking soda. So I was very sober at the end as everyone piled into their vehicles to head home. My lady friend was also very drunk and had apparently gone to bed without my knowledge or even a "good night". Her sister and I cleaned up the mess... empty beer bottles, glassware, napkins, and half-eaten food was everywhere... even outside.

What the hell was I thinking? **Where** in hell did I think this relationship was going? **How** was this life-style even remotely linked with what I enjoyed? **Who** was this idiot that went along with this kind of social behaviour? **When** would I ever get a set of "balls" to speak up; or had I already given up my sense of values? I felt like I had sold my true values and was actually ashamed that I had become so desperate to accept a life-style that was so foreign to me... one that in all honesty I **did not want**!

Am I a person of worth? Apparently not! The next time I spoke to this lady she just asked if I had a good time. She never explained about getting drunk and leaving me to party with unknown strangers. Here was my chance to speak up! But alas, I remained silent. I felt like a coward, unable to stand my ground... a spineless spectacle of a human being; so afraid to offend her. I guess I would have to accept this life-style or simply walk away.

This soon became the "norm" in our relationship. She became the "captain" about all the decisions of what, where, how and why we would be spending time together. At least it was something to do rather than being home alone. I had become a spineless, worthless, complete idiot. But at least there was something to do on the weekends. I would need to drink a good bottle of "courage" to finally stand up and be true to my personal life's values if I expected any changes to happen.

On the weekends, there were sometimes as many as 12 of us going out to eat or going to her girlfriend's cottage to drink or party. There was never *"just the 2 of us"* and this idea was now "water under the bridge". For all intents I had become just a "member of the group".

I had no real attachment to this lady. Unfortunately, I accepted this with a heavy heart. At one point, I finally brought up the fact that I would like it to be just the 2 of us who went out as a couple. She replied with a very bitter tongue... *"You either accept my way of doing things with the people I want to be with, or there is the door!"* It was "her way or the highway".

I hit a low point in my life. I found it hard to let go because I still had someone in my life. I soon discovered that it was merely a *disguise* about what was happening in the real world. I tried to remember that this was **NOT** going to be my final destination and that there would be a brighter future for me. I hoped I would finally realize that I **DID** deserve better. I had but to strive to pull up my socks and get out of a bad situation... to either find someone who actually cared about me... or to accept the fact that I would be alone for the rest of my life. It was time for me to sharpen up!

Granted, I was never the sharpest pencil in the box. I knew what I had to do; but could not do it. I accepted this lady's rules and life-style for many years. I was such a coward but was too scared to be "alone" again. There were many times that she would be too busy for me, or she and her girlfriend would be going away together. When is *Enough totally enough*?

My family and my friends were asking me all the time where she was or what we were doing or why didn't the 2 of get together with them on a weekend. I simply had to reply that she hadn't told me whether or not she was "available". Everyone was asking **when** I was going to stand up to this lady!

The time finally came for the "showdown". I was lucky enough to speak to her on the pretence of the two of us going out together. When I raised this issue, the "fur started to fly". She told me that was NOT going to happen and to just *"suck it up"*. Finally I was man enough to say...*"This is **not** acceptable*"! She simply said... *"There's the door. Good-bye!"*
WHO but myself is to blame for my stupidity? WHY had I fooled myself for so long, believing a change was just around the corner? WHAT had I actually gained from this experience and what had I learned about myself? WHEN had I finally found the courage to speak up and then had to endure so much pain? WHY had I placed myself once again on this plateau of loneliness... in a field of broken hearts and in the land of sorrows?

Granted, I had won the battle; but she had won the war! I was happy and sad at the same moment; for I was without someone in my life. But in reality, I was on my own all along. She was rarely on the scene; nor was she actually interested in my life, my friends nor any future together. It was nothing she had ever wanted to contemplate since the beginning. My mind replayed the events; but my heart could not delete the pain and the sorrow I was experiencing.

Once again, I retreated into my solitary life-style... work... home... and boredom. It was a life that I would now be engaged in for many years to come. As the years rolled by, life did get a little easier as I accepted the way things had become.

So now I thought it was time to get my mind wrapped around more "materialistic" pursuits, rather than a personal pursuit. To say that I handled pain, rejection and isolation very well, was quite evident in the way I **withdrew** from "life".

I just existed... licking my wounds, massaging my heart, wiping away all my tears and wrapping myself in a little ball of insecurity, self-worthlessness and being totally rejected by a relationship gone sour.

Where was this person of worth now? How would I get in touch with my inner strength? Why was I not someone who could find a soul-mate and be happy? How could I improve myself? Why was misery always my constant companion? In reality, I guess having a home in the country was my life preserver. I decided to get involved in some home renovations and landscaping to enhance the beauty and the roadside appeal of my home.

My financial world had definitely improved with my mortgage renewal at at a much lower rate. I could now actually afford to make the payments and buy my own food without relying on my mother's care packages all the time. I could even have some "play money" left over.

I had also received a very nice pay raise at work. My employer said... *"You are now an asset to the company. Both your work experience and your increased knowledge of the firm's business has been recognized by management. We feel you have totally earned our respect in your ability to contribute to the firm's profit. A pay raise is your reward for all your hard work."*

So with a brighter financial world, this was a positive step in my life. Yes, I had worked for it; but to actually have my boss exclaim that I

was "worthy" of the pay increase lifted my inner spirit to a new plateau of self-assurance, worthiness and gave a different slant to my life's direction. Now I would be able to do some home improvements as a "release" after work.

My social life was non-existent and that was okay since I seemed to have a way of turning all that part of my life into a "sham".

So I began to look for a carpenter. My abilities with a hammer were not within my range of possibility. My father had absolutely no desire or interest in helping me learns ANY carpentry skills. If my mother got on his case, he would grudgingly create the item I wanted. He would NOT allow me to watch or learn any method of how to do things properly.

Since grandfather had been very gifted in carpentry; my father had a good trainer. Too bad for me that my father never had any inclination or desire to pass along any of the skills he had learned. The only time he wanted to be in my company was when he had a "job" he wanted me to do for him or help him with something he had undertaken. Then I was useful. Otherwise, I was to be out of sight and out of his way. This was his preferred method of handling my "existence" in the family.

Having lived in a small city, word of mouth was always the best way to find someone who knew and could recommend someone for my home improvement needs. So I went into the local grocery store and talked to people. This was my new "mission". As a matter of fact, on my first visit to the store, I actually found a man who knew some locals with the skills and the work ethics to do the job I needed.

I decided to build a large wooden deck at the rear of my home. First of all, because the one already there needed replacing; and second... the one there was very small for any real purpose. If a new deck were there, it would allow me to watch and observe the "carpenter's skills" and his work ethic to ensure his standard of building was up to my expected results.

It turned out to be a "new world" of enjoyment for me as well. He allowed me both to participate in the building of the deck and he explained why he was doing what he was and why he was doing it "that way". It was a win-win experience and I took pride in my little bit of "hands-on" in the completion of this project.

I had found a skilled workman that I knew I could rely on and together we had build a new bond of friendship between us. Because I had already saved the money to build this deck, future improvements would follow.

This experience gave me a sense of accomplishment as well as increasing the real estate value of my home. Now I took a look at the exterior grounds. I knew it would help release any stress from work and would also help fill in my free time. I took great pleasure in learning about the horticultural products that I had hoped to plant... their care and the proper placement of them in my yard.

The long hours I spent working in the yard were totally rewarding, as I looked back each day at the work already completed. In fact I was pretty proud of myself for all the transformation that had happened so far. All too soon, my internal and exterior work projects all seem to have come to fruition. Although I was pleased with the work done, I started to despair about what I could do now to occupy my free time.

How was I going to fill all this free time after work? I had no hobbies, had never made any room for friendships; had never really connected with any of the people I worked with. I had nobody who would be interested in dropping over for a visit. *I WAS LOST!*

I hadn't even realized that several years had passed; but loneliness was beginning to play havoc with my mind and my senses were starting to affect my outlook on life. Questions began to run through my mind... *How am I going to cope? How can I keep from going mad? When will some inspiration start to kick in? Who am I now? Why am I here? Why don't I see any significance at all to my life?*

It was almost as if I were praying. I guess I simply had to open my mind and have a positive attitude and things may happen for a greater good. A new lady had started to work as a receptionist at our office. Shades of "horror" flew across my mind. Was I in my "right mind"? Was there a message to take yet another "chance"?

I remember many years ago, dating a former employee and all the heartache, all the misery and all the pain that I endured. For many years I could not face reality... or myself. There was so much pain from this ordeal.

I decided that **my** life was going nowhere fast. But yet... life was going along without me! Maybe a slow and sure approach should be used in any attempt to take the first tentative step towards a date. I knew absolutely nothing about this new lady so I was patient.

I started to pay more attention to the people in the office... especially during coffee break discussions. Previously I would have had coffee at my desk; sometimes persuaded to join someone for a coffee break to discuss a work problem. It was soon noticed that my presence at coffee break was becoming "the norm" and there was less comment about "the other man" now at our coffee breaks. I tried to shrug off the questioning comments... saying things like... *"I needed to stretch my legs."*

I tried to make it a point to sit near the new lady, in an attempt to overhear any snippet of conversation about her life. Eventually, I became bold. I asked the ladies if I could join them on a regular basis and take part in their discussions. I also said that I had some ideas to share about what was going on with management and some of the decisions that were going to be made.

I was both proud and ashamed of myself for this step and I was not too happy being an "office informer" of upcoming policy/staff changes. However, on the positive side, I was now part of the "group" of ladies who were in my personal section of the office and the new lady was part of this group.

Since the ladies felt I was "on the inside" I was quite often asked to join them at coffee break. They felt that there may be a chance that I might be able to help them when something new might be forthcoming. Of course, I threw my 2 cents in when there were discussions about family and/or office gossip.

I also had to be very careful in group discussions and certainly did not want to dominate any part of it. I tried to make it a point to be walking back at the same time as the new lady was heading back to her desk; but did not want to draw any attention to that fact at all.

On occasion she would make a point of asking a question pertaining to a work assignment that she had been given and what the "proper procedure" would be to complete the task. The other women also now turned their attention to me for any answers they may need. Because I was now part of the "group" and they felt "comfortable" in approaching me for help, I would respond with the "correct" answer... or if I were in doubt, I said I would get back to them with the answer.

What a great idea this was. It would give me a logical reason to be at her work station and hopefully explaining everything would give me a few more minutes spending time with her.
"Home" was where the hurt was; so I was the master of my own destination. The ball was in **my** court. I had to either stand up to the plate or remain an "onlooker" from the benches.

It was **my** problem and mine alone, to solve this dilemma about how to get up closer and personal with this lady. I just needed the nerves to kick in for me to be brave enough to ask about the possibility of an "after-work" drink.

<u>WHY</u> was this not a good idea? <u>HOW</u> will I know the right time has come to ask her out? <u>WHAT</u> should I do or say so I won't embarrass myself if she's not interested? <u>WHERE</u> should I take her for "the drink" if the answer is "yes"? <u>WHO</u> or what should we talk about? I was so out of step with good conversation that I felt totally out of my element.

All of these questions and comments kept running through my mind whenever I was near this lady. I couldn't ask her out until I got a grip on my emotions, so my brain could actually work the way it was supposed to. Days would turn into weeks and I was beginning to feel like a real coward and a failure... yet again.

Finally the day arrived when she called me to her desk to clarify a job procedure that she didn't feel confident about the right course she should be taking. I told myself... *"It's now or never chum! Get a grip! Have some confidence in your own ability!"* Luckily I knew the correct answer to her question and she thanked me for my promptness and for the clarification about the project.

As I was leaving her work station, I turned around and from somewhere inside myself, I asked her if she would like to meet after work for a drink if possible. It seemed like forever; but in reality, her response was given quite quickly. She said she would consider the request. Because she had been divorced for a year, she hadn't given much thought about a date or how she felt about such an offer.

I told her there was no pressure at all and would gladly allow her all the time she might need to think about it. When she was ready and comfortable, she could let me know how she felt. Surprisingly, she thanked me for my kindness and I walked away.

In my own mind, I wasn't at all sure if I had asked her properly; if I was too vague; if it seemed that I didn't care whether she came or not. I did hope that I showed genuine interest in receiving a positive response and hoped that my request didn't put me in a "bad light". Time will tell; let the chips fall where they may. I had done my best.

It was about 3 weeks later that she approached me for another job-related question. In reality, she already knew the answer; but she was looking for a private moment. She willingly expressed her interest in meeting me after work for a drink at a nearby bar and grill. She said that she was "analyzing" my attitude at work about whether I was changing or was I just the same kind of person I always was. I didn't realize she was "testing" me; but apparently I had passed and a date and time were arranged for us to meet outside work.

It was hard to contain myself with the excitement of this new success. I was thrilled that I had merely found the courage to have asked her out in the first place.

It really blew my mind that it really wasn't that difficult. I had overcome my anxiety and lack of confidence in myself and all was good. We met at the location she had chosen, in separate cars so we wouldn't draw any undue attention that we were having a drink together. I also think in her mind, that it was a security issue for her and that was okay too.

My fears were palpable: what to talk about; how to pick the place; what to ask... had all been for naught. She had taken control of the situation and had made the choices: the time, the place... even started the conversation. I listened and sometimes added my own comments.

All my fretting and sleepless nights turned out to be a total waste of my time. In the end, I was so happy and relieved that I began to relax. I was able to relate and to share in all the discussions, hoping I didn't sound "unintelligent" or "unreasonable" in my comments. I could not believe how comfortable I was in her company and the ease in which we enjoyed a conversation on many diverse subjects.

It was like we had had several conversations before... even to the point of sharing answers. It was almost like we had been together in another time and place and now we were "re-united" and just seemed to pick up where we had left off "the last time". I was enjoying this time so much and as the saying goes... *"Time stands still for no one. Like a Timex watch, it just keeps on ticking."*

I could not believe that neither I nor the young lady had realized that 2 hours had passed so quickly. As we scrambled to say our good-byes, I asked if we might do this again soon. I felt that we had already established a bond of friendship and I truly wanted to see how far this new connection would go. She also said that she felt very comfortable and was glad she had trusted her "gut instinct" to be correct about me and that my intentions were genuine. Consequently, she agreed that we could meet again and possibly for a walk in the local park on the weekend.

For me, the weekend seemed like an eternity away. For some reason the hours dragged slowly along. Like "Murphy's Law"... the more you hope things will go a certain way; the more they tend to go the opposite way. In reality, this was not the case, whatsoever. It was the excitement of being with this lady; going for that walk on the weekend that took total control of my brain for the rest of the week. However, what I had accomplished at work seemed a total blur.

We had exchanged phone numbers at work to keep prying eyes and ears from knowing what was going on, in order for us to confirm the time for our walk and where in the park that we could meet. She actually called me at home that very Friday night to say that it would have to be a late afternoon walk because her children had made plans for her during the early part of the day. I told her I was totally flexible in the time and we set our plans in place and she thanked me for being understanding.

I was very anxious to see her again and I arrived ahead of the "prescribed" time, wanting to have a few minutes to think about things we might share in our conversation. I did not see her approaching because I was deep in thought and when she caught my attention, she just laughed. *"You look like an expectant father"* she said... *"pacing back and forth. What in the world was so serious to cause such gestures that I saw you showing?*

At this point, I asked myself **what** was I thinking. **What** was I going to get involved in? **Why** did I now want to take a chance with a new relationship? **Who** would potentially be the one that would be hurt if this attempt continues? **When** would I know if I was doing the right thing for my life? **Where** did I hope this new relationship would take me? **How** was this the right step for me? Should I be doing some more serious thinking before I jumped in with both feet?

At this point, reality kicked in! I decided that it was much too late at this point to start second-guessing myself or my actions. I just quickly smiled in recognition of her arrival and told her that I was thinking of things that we might chat about on our walk.

I did NOT tell her what my brain was telling me. She quickly asked... *"So what have you decided we should talk about as we walk this afternoon?"* I was really caught off guard. My true thoughts were of "myself" and about the "present circumstances" I was in. So I went deep inside and thought of a compliment to give her. I told her that she looked very nice and I was really happy to see her and to have some time to get to know her a little better.

She smiled and it appeared that my tiny brain had come up with the perfect response and I was now "off the hook". We walked and talked for what seemed like hours; but I was totally at ease and perfectly comfortable about everything we chatted about. I actually came up with some ideas myself, which surprised me a little.

She asked the time and both of us were amazed... even a little shocked... so we quickly reversed our steps and increased our pace to get us back to the parking lot and our cars. I asked if she would like to join me for dinner later that evening or the next day and she responded that the next day would work out better for her. She said she would have to leave a meal ready for her kids when she went out. I thought this comment made her a very responsible parent. Her plans had to come secondary to their needs; so she certainly scored points with me.

As I was driving home, my "grey matter" started its own *thinking process.* All the questions that had been running through my head while I was waiting for her. Again... was I doing the right thing? Was this the course of action that a logical, reasonable man should be doing? I know I was very lonely and unhappy with my current life; so I quickly got over my concerns and doubts. It was about time that I did something for ME. I needed to seek out happiness so the depression wouldn't get a strangle hold on my life.

I decided a more "positive" outlook would be far more beneficial than to strangle in negativity. When I sat down and actually examined the facts about our time together today, I realized I had totally enjoyed myself. I was not yet in a "committed" relationship.

It was merely a couple of new friends enjoying time together... getting to know likes and dislikes; looking for common ground to help build something positive in the future.

We went out the next evening. I picked out a "low-light", romantic environment, with good quality food. This whole effort was an attempt to set a positive atmosphere for the rest of the evening. She had arrived in her own car and said she was very pleased with my choice. We ordered wine and some good food and soon the conversation flowed.

Both of us seemed very interested in the interchange of our opinions on a variety of subjects and the evening was slowly drifting along. All too soon our evening together was drawing to a close. I walked her to her car and the difficult moment of a possible "kiss good night" was upon us. She sensed this and was pleased that I had not pushed in an attempt to kiss her. So she made the move to kiss me on "her terms" and a promise to talk on the phone the very next day.

WHERE was I going in this quest? WHAT was this emotion within me, now taking control? WHEN would I know if I was doing the right thing? WHY was now the right time, the right lady, the right path to be heading down? Was this the possible future that I had so longed to find? WHO would or could help me in my decision? I had no confidence in my ability to make the right decisions any more. I had been wrong many times and was now totally afraid that my brain and my heart were not working together. It seemed they were at opposite ends of the spectrum of logic, common sense and yes, even love.

I did receive a phone call the next day from her to thank me for a lovely dinner and evening. I told her that I too had totally enjoyed her company, the conversation and the time we spent together. I ended the call telling her that I would like to spend more time with her because I could sense a close bond becoming very real in such a short time. To my surprise, she too said that she felt comfortable with me as well; that I was not too assertive and she liked that I respected her opinion. She said it was very refreshing since her ex-husband had never allowed her to express an opinion about anything.

It was always "his way" or "the highway". Once more we made plans to have another walk in the middle of the coming week, to get to know one another more. She also said how much she appreciated the time to go slowly. This was also a new experience for her and she didn't want to rush into any possible relationship too soon. I agreed and told her I wanted us to take our time to discover more about one another and to form a good foundation of respect and understanding before anything else.

WHAT kind of thoughts was she having? Were they positive or negative? WHEN did she feel she might be totally comfortable enough to let down any barriers that may still be in place? WHY was she having doubting thoughts? <u>WHERE</u> her thoughts of the future there were might be for us? <u>WHO</u> might she turn to for advice? She appeared to be a very strong-minded woman; or was this just an act of "self-protection" from letting down her guard too soon?

Again, we met for a walk in the local park on Wednesday of the next week. Surprisingly, we both arrived at the same time and both of us exclaimed how glad we were to be together again here, instead of at the office. We were now both very open and honest with each other and getting into more personal topics. This was better than general conversation about world topics or talking about office gossip.

We were beginning to share with one another about our previous relationships and what we felt might have gone wrong in the breakdown. We both felt quite comfortable about talking about this and about the decisions we made to bail out of these relationships. We had been pushed to the "brink of despair"... far beyond what was realistic or "normal".

At this point, I am not sure which of us reached out first to hold hands, as we continued walking without breaking our conversation. It just seemed like the "natural course of action". It was becoming very obvious that a new bond had been formed and each of us seemed willing to enter this new relationship.

For the first time in a very long time, my heart felt alive and the heavy weight of doubt was being lifted from my shoulders. Was I starting to feel some real happiness... a feeling that had been lost for many years... and was now being rekindled in this new relationship?

<u>WHAT</u> was this pleasant feeling that I was now experiencing? <u>WHERE</u> had it been hiding all this time? <u>WHY</u> was this new, refreshing feeling of life... of being alive... of being aware of everything around me happening now? <u>WHO</u> and what was I becoming? I actually felt like a person of worth for the first time in a long time. I was dumbfounded

by this feeling. <u>WHEN</u> would I awake and realize it was not reality; but only a dream?

Something was happening to me; something I had prayed long and hard for over many years. Was I now to awake from this dream and my "old world" would be there to greet me with unhappiness and despair?

We became very aware of the time and because we were so wrapped up in our conversation, and did not realize that time had NOT stopped, time kept marching forward. But we both realized that we had found happiness in each other's company and neither of us wanted this time to end. But of course, it must!

But we had forged a bond; we had made a commitment to one another and life had been renewed for us. There is an aphorism that simply states: *"The nicest thing about the future is that it always starts tomorrow."* and another one states" *"Always be yourself because the people don't mind and the ones who mind, don't matter."*

Both of these statements really ring true for me because I felt like I indeed, had a future and I was truly happy to be now looking forward to tomorrow and every tomorrow following. The other true fact that had surfaced was that I had been "myself" in her company. The saying goes... *"what you see is what you get"*. She had respected and appreciated my sincerity. The "true me" is what she was seeing and she had a total understanding of my "make-up" and my somewhat "crazy" character. Everything was good and that was all that mattered.

<u>WHAT</u> if? Was this truly a new beginning... a new chapter opening up in my life? <u>WHY</u> had now become the appropriate time for this relationship to have been formed? <u>WHO</u> was I kidding? I was thrilled that this opportunity had presented itself and it was up to me to do my utmost, to make this relationship work! <u>WHERE</u> in my mind was I thinking that this was positive and not negative?

WHEN would my brain kick in? My heart was currently speaking for my body. Shouldn't I be seeking my brain for the logic and common sense about this new relationship and where it might be taking me? Was I prepared to overcome all those "speed bumps" in life for this new relationship? Would I now have a "committed" partner to help smooth them out?

We were more connected with each other and we regularly talked on the phone as well as chatted with each other at the office. But seeing one another in a more "professional" atmosphere was also an uplifting experience. I do believe I had a brighter smile and a quicker step and a whole lot better outlook on life now.

It was time for me to meet her children. Till now, they had only heard about me; but they saw that their Mother was a much happier person because I was in her life. So a weekend dinner for all of us was to be the order of the day. I was on pins and needles with this new experience looming on the horizon.

But I quickly realized that their mother had somewhat prepared them for our meeting. When the night arrived, I arrived with a dozen roses and a couple of bottles of wine as a "thank you" for the invitation to dinner. Because I knew her children were older, I was hoping they might also share a glass of wine with the meal. I was pleasantly surprised when her daughter opened the door and welcomed me into their home.

Her son was watching a game on TV and just "waved" his arm in the air to recognize my arrival. So far; so good. Their mother greeted me with a kiss in front of them with a happy smile, in recognition of my arrival.

I also think it was to reassure me that all was well in the household and there was no "anger or hostility". Consequently I felt the pressure I had been feeling about this experience had been lifted off my shoulders. My mind had prepared me for a totally different reception and now I could relax and "be myself". All was well in this environment! I offered my assistance in the kitchen and was told since I was a guest to go and watch the game with her son.

She and her daughter had all the preparations well in hand. However, she did allow me to open the wine and pour a glass for everyone. Her son was too wrapped up in the game for any conversation; so I took the liberty of sitting on the couch, sipping my wine and surveying the contents of the house. I wanted to be able to start a conversation about something that might have caught my eye. I thought this would make me a "good boy scout"... being prepared and all that. I didn't want to be caught off guard if I were asked a question.

I was truly thankful that the dinner conversation was started when she asked the kids about what concerned them about their days' activities. I sat and watched how "masterfully" she calmed their concerns and even asked my opinion about some of the things she had said, inviting me into the conversation and the family as a whole.

I was very pleased to be included in the conversation; but was very aware not to over-step the boundaries, about inserting my opinion too strongly. However, I did try to add my thoughts in a respectful way, to show I was interested in the topic. But I also finished with the phrase... "Mother knows best"... and her advice was quite sound in my judgement.

After dinner, we played a couple of board games and chatted about many subjects... primarily about what the kids were up to; school work and the relationships they were involved in with their "significant others". For the first time, I was happy to be in a family atmosphere once again. But this family was a loving family and I felt like I had arrived at "my new home". I had been welcomed and brought "into the fold".

The kids' dates arrived and soon she and I were alone... to clean up after dinner; doing the dishes and so forth. We felt like true "partners"... each willing to help the other. When we finished, we poured another glass of wine and sat on the couch, totally relaxed with each other. All was very right with our world.

She said that she had been a little concerned about how the dinner would turn out; but said her kids had given her the "thumbs up" sign in approval and said they would have left a lot earlier if they had not totally accepted me!

We made plans for another walk and a drive in the country for the next day and with a kiss goodnight at the doorway, I was off home, to relive the evening and the family connection that I had experienced. My brain was working overtime, with all these new experiences and wondering where on earth this new relationship was heading. Was I sure this is where I wanted to go?

WHO was I becoming? WHY was there this new sense of "self-worth"? WHEN would I know if I was experiencing reality and not just a moment of being happy in a relationship; but wanting this new and refreshing inner feeling to keep going? Please do not break this bubble of make believe! WHERE did my future lay before me? WHAT was happening to my solitary life-style... not that I wasn't happy with it; but it was and had been a "constant" in my life... something I was familiar with (not necessarily happy with) but at least I knew of its existence and had accepted it .

For the first time, I knew I was really scared! I was looking at a new beginning, a new life, a new partner, a new family unit, a whole new environment of change, of being a "willow tree"... willing to bend in all situations; not to be an oak, unable to bend with any new scenario that could now be throwing speed bumps in my direction.

Would I, or did I know myself, how I should or could react with these new life experiences. **How** best could I calm the wild waters of tension or distress?

It was not just me anymore; but there was a new partner and her children that would be entering my world. **Was** I up to the task? **Would** I be able to comprehend the right course of action? **Would** I fail miserably? **Would** self-doubt now be my new companion? **Would** I or could I ever truly relay on my new companion for her logic and good common sense, to steer me in the right direction?

Would we be at "logger-heads" with each other about the correct way to handle our problems? Would she want my input when it came to her children? To be honest, I lacked any experience dealing with teenagers and how they saw their lives. They knew their mother's concern and the way she handled the situations was the norm in their lives.

Had this evening I had just enjoyed been a night of "good manners"... one that was not real but merely an evening they had "put on a good front" so that things would go well for their mother's sake? <u>WHEN</u> would this prove out NOT to be the normal acceptance of life? Would the reality be total mass confusion? <u>WHAT</u> would I do then?

<u>WHERE</u> would my "safe" haven be? Would it even possibly exist in the first place? <u>WHY</u> was I now "second-guessing myself? Whose voice was I hearing in my head?

To say that my night's sleep was peaceful would be a total, flat-out lie! I tossed and turned for the whole night, fighting every thought that came to light; trying my best to interject logic and common sense. I constantly fought negative thoughts. This unsure, non-reliant, unstable, inner being could seemingly NOT make a decision to save his own sanity or even have a good night's sleep.

Eventually I fell into a very light sleep, waking up totally exhausted and feeling for the first time "uneasy" with this new direction my life had taken. I felt totally torn; as though I was now two separate people... or at least that my brain had 2 separate components... both fighting for dominance!

I called and set a time to pick her up for our walk and drive through the country that we had planned for the next day. I told her of my previous sleepless night and how I was fighting with myself to know that I was doing the right thing. I also said that there was still some "self-doubt" and that I wanted to be totally honest and upfront with her.

She sat there in silence... which seemed like an eternity; but in reality was only a few moments. She said... *"I am glad you are being honest with me about your feelings. Perhaps you should now take me home and give yourself enough time to feel sure, not only about your feelings for me but about the new relationship with me and my children. Apparently this needs to be figured out before we can move forward."*

I was frozen... dead in my tracks, because I openly spoke about my concerns, I had abruptly ended any new relationship! My new "life's choice had instantly vanished! The happiness and contentment that had been my life's quest for so long... for a life-partner to share all life's ups and downs had now disappeared.

My inner peace of mind knowing that I might have a "soul-mate" as an anchor in the rough seas of life... someone to give her opinions, to smooth out the rough edges and to find winning solutions that were unclear to me, was now LOST. I was all alone, just like before... like a lonely "floating bottle", alone on the rough seas of life.

I was totally taken aback with her response; but then realized I had backed her into a corner unknowingly, by the very words I had spoken. I realized I should have taken more time with my own inner emotional state, before opening my big mouth. Now I had to suffer the consequences of my actions. I was now between "a rock and a hard place" in a struggle with my own decision about the "right path" for my life.

Seeing her in the office the next morning, she walked by me with only a simple smile. Almost instantly, it was like a knife had been driven through my body and only "death" was the end result of this simple act. I did not know how to react.

My inner emotions were like a volcano... erupting inside my head. Work would have to be put on the back burner. My main priority was "saving my sanity" and hopefully being able to come to the right course of action with this new relationship... the quest for the happiness in life that I was seeking.

It was a very long week, being in her company at the office... although only at a distance. The heavy weight of despair that had overtaken me was almost too much to bear. As I walked passed her on my way out the door at the end of the day, a simple "good night" came from my lips and an almost "ice cold" response was given as she responded... *"with you too".*

This was a totally painful experience; one I needed to get used to, or find the true inner feeling that I thought was there in the first place. Then I would need to apologize and hopefully rediscover happiness and contentment in my life. It would be a long and sleepless weekend of "rediscovering, refining, weighing the pros and cons of my concerns" and hopefully know what I must do (or not do), to be in control of the path for my life.

WHAT had I done to myself? WHAT indeed? WHY was I now having second thoughts about my feelings for this lady? WHO was I fooling? Nobody but myself! WHERE did I think, in my wildest dreams, that my life's path was now going back to despair, to unhappiness, to loneliness... to a life that I had not really been part of; but just going through the motions of getting up, putting in my time in the office and going home to four walls that surround me? WHEN would I come to my senses... about being honest with myself; of totally realizing that I had experienced happiness; that there was a real bond to another human being; of totally feeling alive and actually looking forward to that companionship and love with a purpose in mind?

Most of all, I was looking forward to having the support from someone who actually had my best interests at heart; not merely "going through the motions" of seeing what they could get out of the experience.

Life does NOT promise happiness, contentment and a fulfilment of all your dreams. You have to work at it every single day. Having a partner who "has your back" and your best interests at heart to help you succeed in your dreams and is a part of your life, doesn't get any better than that! I felt foolish for my actions of the previous week; of opening my mouth and speaking words that were hurtful for her to hear about being unsure of having a relationship with her and not using the brain God had given me, to apply logic and common sense before speaking. If I had been more aware, I could have been in a better place than the spot that I was now in.

WHEN could I arrange a time and place with her to help clear the air? WHAT would be her response to my request for a talk? WHY would she even grant me this request? WHO did I think I was, to be able to hurt her like I did and then think that all would be forgiven? Was I really that naive? Where would the opportunity present itself? Would it be in the workplace? I told myself that was "idiotic".

I would call her privately to see if she would meet me for a walk in the park. Maybe I could better judge my chances of a possible reunion. It all depended on the reception I got once I had the opportunity to be with her.

I gathered my courage on Sunday night. Truly, this was going to be one of the hardest phone calls I would ever make. Not knowing the response at the other end, sent a chill up my spine. The result of this call would either *make* or *break* my future of potential happiness with this lady.

When she answered the phone, there was very little to say at the beginning and her tone was quite cool. I told her first of all, that

I wanted to apologize for my words and my hesitation about our relationship. I asked to be forgiven and said that even if she did not want to give me a second chance, I hoped we might still be friends. Maybe we could at least enjoy a coffee break or a walk in the park at some point.

I hoped she would agree to meet me for a walk, and talk about our issues and clear the air about any doubts she may have about my true intentions. I hoped she could see the pain of losing her in my life and the effect it was having on me emotionally. I really needed this chance to make amends! Dead silence followed, for what seemed to be an eternity! I was sure she was going to hang up; but hopefully she would be polite enough to at least say she was no longer interested. At that point I would know if I blown any kind of relationship out of the water!

My heart jumped for joy as I heard her voice... a softer tone, a more gentle tone, a more understanding tone. Then she agreed to meet me for a walk and a talk. She said that she did not want to break this connection we were building because it seemed like a good one.

She also wanted me to realize that it was up to ME to decide both our fates! She said... *"This cannot be taken lightly and you have to be totally on board before we can enter a relationship. If it is to be built on love, trust, caring and wanting to build a life together, it can never be a one-sided affair."*

I had to know my true self; what I wanted in our relationship. I had to go in with my eyes wide open to having her... her children and a totally new beginning for us both. It was almost like instant relief... a second chance... a chance to enjoy a renewed happiness! The following Monday at work, I could hardly wait for her to come in; to see her and know that we had re-connected and that a pleasant *"good morning"* and a smile would be there to greet me as my reward. I motioned to her to come to my desk pretending I had a work-related issue to discuss.

In reality, I wanted to speak to her to arrange our walk and talk timetable and to personally tell her how sorry I was for my previous comments about our relationship. Finally, I wanted to say how happy I was, to be getting a "second chance" at a relationship and I hoped we were now going forward toward a future together. I was not disappointed because she gave me a big *hello* and a beautiful smile which seemed to fill my office space.

I was happy and feeling "alive" once again. I had a purpose in life and my inner feelings were coming "alive". She suggested a short walk right after work, to clear the air and remove any doubtful feelings and to once again, get "in sync" with each other's emotions. We also made plans for more regular conversations in the future. I was thrilled to say the least.

It was like I had been in this terrible dream and was now awakening. She was going to be a big part of my life and for me, life was now *rich and full!* Somehow I was not able to function very well throughout the work day because my thoughts were on our walk after work and my re-connection with her was my only true thought for the rest of the day!

I could hardly wait for the end of the day. The clock seemed to be in slow-motion. But it was soon time for us to meet. I was both pleased and surprised when she gave me a kiss *hello*... and I was on top of the world! She said she was glad I had come to my senses because she had already felt a real commitment but was shocked that I was hesitant.

I said I was not really concerned about "our" commitment; but was a little concerned about having an "instant" family under one roof. To be honest, I was a little worried about my own personal coping skills. How would I adjust to this new life-style and would our personal relationship be put to a test? At this point, she just laughed and I looked at her in total amazement.

She said that her daughter was off to University and her son was going to College. Yes, he would be living with us; but with school and after school employment, a girlfriend and time with his buddies, we would scarcely see him at home. She wondered why I hadn't even considered any of this.

It was like a weight had been lifted off my shoulders. All my concerns and worries about dealing with her two adult children, were not even issues to be considered at all. I threw up my arms! *What was I thinking?* I smiled at her and again said how sorry I was about any doubts I may have had. I reaffirmed my love and my emotional feelings for her.

At this point, she grasped my hand in hers... the bond had been re-cemented. We could see a life together in our future and all was right with my world.

WHY had I not been able in the first place to have figured this out? WHO was this person inside my body... but merely a big fool? WHAT had I put myself through for no logical reason since fear had been the ruler of my mind and my weekend was sleepless and miserable? WHEN would I have awakened to rationalizing the facts of this new relationship and weighed the pros and cons of the whole thing? WHERE would I have been in life, if she had not given me this second chance at happiness?

I was indeed a fortunate man to have such an understanding new partner in my life. I knew instantly that I was in the right space and the right time of my life's existence. My world was now orbiting on its proper axis; the speed bumps of worry, concern and uncertainty had all vanished. My world was now at it should have been all along! As we walked along, hand in hand, I felt like a man who had won the lottery; only THIS was better! We had cleared the air of all my concerns and now we plotted the next course of action we should take.

Together, we were now a "formidable" force to be reckoned with and our future was the road we were now on... no doubts, no fears, but strictly this bond of connection to each other and we were a "team" from this point onwards! She and her son moved in with me the very next weekend, as a statement of our commitment to each other and to the world. We were in fact... *a family unit* .

For the first time in a lot of years, I was truly and completely happy. My life had finally "come together" and I had a family in my life on a full-time basis. Of course, she was correct! Her son was barely there. Except for an occasional meal with us, he was usually just passing through on his way to his room or out the door. For the most part, we were a couple... enjoying the time we shared after the day at work. It all seemed so "normal"; like we had been doing this for years. It did not seem like a new, beginning environment at all.

Weeks turned into years of happy memories and I did not want this happiness to ever end. But life had other plans for our destiny to be changed! We had been on a wonderful European holiday to celebrate my retirement from work. Unfortunately she still had a few years to put in before she could retire.

It was like a veil had been drawn almost instantly after our return from a holiday. Her health was starting to suffer. She was always feeling like she had a flu virus every day and her strength and stamina were declining on a daily basis as well. Her doctor was puzzled and tried many different methods and tests to come up with a solution; but there was nothing.

Her doctor had been at her wits end and it was time to see a specialist. Again more tests were carried out and still the misery continued. Many specialists... one after another were brought in and still not one of them could point a finger at the cause and none of them were ever in agreement!

Finally we got to a specialist who basically said with a cold heart... *"If I had to bet on anything, I'd bet you had cancer."* We both sat there stunned with this statement; both of our eyes filled with tears and our hearts became rock heavy in our bodies. The world had come to a crashing halt! *WHAT HORROR!*

She had always been "my rock" in my world of solidarity. Now the wheels had turned and it was my turn to be "her rock; her comfort" and do my utmost best to do all I could... to never let her feel she was on her own in this horrific battle. We were a team and damn it... we would explore any and all avenues to try and beat this disease!

We became "regulars" at the cancer clinic, going through the necessary cancer treatments. I was always trying to put on a "false face" that we were going to "overcome". Because she was a strong-willed lady, she acknowledged my positive attitude and a positive outcome was our goal.

I had seen the cancer environment. To be honest, I was not as sure as I put on, that we were going to beat cancer. God forgive me; but I didn't believe that we were going to "win".
She was getting weaker daily and her skin colour was changing to a grey tone; her appetite was declining and the pain level was constantly increasing! She was only able to remain at home for two more years with home assistance. Soon even that was not possible.

She spent another year and a half in the cancer hospital so that morphine could be given to her as required. Even then she was going downhill and in so much pain. For the final six months, she was in a palliative care unit and the doctor said her time was closing in. But he promised she would have all the morphine she needed to alleviate the pain.

When I entered her room, she smiled and I tried my best to smile back. I continued to try and be as strong for her as she had always been for me. I would crawl up in bed with her...just to be close and hold her. I wanted to let her know my love for her was strong and that she was still my whole world!

How this lady had the strength and ability to orchestrate her own upcoming funeral arrangements demonstrates her strength of conviction. She knew I would be a "basket– case"... which I was. She took control and made the arrangements she wanted... the flowers, the music and the service to be conducted. She loved me so much that she spared me these details. How lucky was I to be *loved this much by such a special lady!!!*

I received a phone call shortly after midnight that it was time for me to get to the hospital... to be there for her in her last minutes. How I was able to drive there with tear-filled eyes is a mystery. It must have been God's divine intervention to get me there safely; to be her comfort at the end; to share a final kiss, a hug and a few parting words about our love for one another. Then she was gone! I felt her spirit leave her body; I prayed for her to take me with her! My heart is hers! My world is nothing without her! I have no will or desire to stay; I am truly lost! I felt as if my own body were dying and yet, I sat at the bedside... tears flowing freely; my body trembling in shock.

My world exploded inside my head! My desire to live was no longer an "emotional feeling". I was a totally shattered human being.

WHAT has just happened to me? WHAT horrific pain has now overtake my heart and my body? WHOSE was this shattered soul that is now occupying my body? I did not feel as if I were in possession of my body at all. I thought I was merely a *"heavenly spirit"* that was adrift in this world, wanting to follow my lady who has just died.

WHERE was my happy world of contentment with my special lady now? Even though she was very ill, I could reach out, squeeze her hand, run my hand over her face as an acknowledgement that I was there by her side, re-enforcing my bond of love with her. WHEN would God also take me to be reunited with her spirit for all eternity?

WHY did He take the love of my life from me? WHAT had I done to displease Him with my life's action here on earth? WHY was I not entitled to have happiness in my life? WHY had God given me this beautiful lady in my life, in the first place... only to take her from me now? WHY did God choose to take her, when I told Him to please take "me" in her place?

I was willing to give my life for her. Without her in my life I no longer had a reason to live. She had children to watch as they grew in life... their careers, marriages and even grandchildren to enjoy.

WHEN would this pain of her loss not feel so intense? I truly wanted to die and not be in this world any longer. I wanted to join her and feel her love again. WHAT would now be come of me? WHAT was the purpose in going on... adrift in the rough seas of life? My beautiful lady who was my anchor in life; my support and my guide to steer me from harm... was no longer there. I need her through every moment of indecision in my life.

I knew I must put pen to paper to create a poem in her memory and to write a book as a tribute to her life and everything that she touched with her existence in this world. I knew how terrible her loss would be felt by all those who were blessed to know her and have felt her touch their lives.

This was also kind of a "selfish" moment on my part; to help heal my shattered heart. I still felt a strong bond of connection to her; as though I still had her in my life. Most definitely she was in my mind and my heart and would be for the rest of my life. The book I wrote as a "legacy to her memory" and for all those who in a small way could get to know her strengths, her commitment to life and the love that I was so blessed to receive from her is entitled... *"Now You Have Her... Now You Don't".*

The poem I wrote to express my love to her, my emotional state, my hope to be reunited with her upon my death and the happiness and joy that she brought to my life follows...

My Love Is Forever

I was once blessed with love
the feeling of closeness to you.
You were my gift from God above,
to have the whole day through.

Now my life is changed...
no longer safe in my arms;
your time has come to leave me.
My sense of worth removed.
The void of closeness to you
now fills my world completely.
I must now search my memories
for your love I surely need.

Rest now my lady;
my love will never die.
I know we will be together;
we will always live forever.
Our minds will be connected
through all eternity.

I was now totally alone... scared of the world. My survivor skills had been diminished and I was left to figure out **how** to cope with this hole in my heart. My body's spirit was broken and a life and future was ahead of me but I really did not want to be a part of it any more. I did what any wounded animal does. I took refuge in a place where I felt safe... in a world of solitude. My mind only wanted to think of the past and did not really want to connect to the world in any way.

Again, as before, I went through the motions of living. I worked to support myself and dreaded each and every day I faced, with no particular interest in what was going on in the world. I closed my mind to the huge and horrific loss I had just felt. My soul-mate and my life's partner was no longer part of my world. I was now **totally** alone once again!

For years I was a hermit... although a "modern-day" hermit. I was part of the world for the required number of hours that were needed to perform at my job. But once that was done, it was back to my world of solitude and withdrawing from a world in which I had absolutely no interest. Time was going by very slowly for me. Life was a drudgery. Nothing in my present nor my future had any importance in my life. What was really the point of even "being here" in the first place?

My dear mother, who was now my only real, personal contact was expressing her concerns for my "mental" state and my physical well-being. I told Mom of my concerns about life and all the pain that had been thrown in my direction. I promised her I would NOT do anything "stupid"... like commit suicide. But the pain of my loss was as fresh now as if it had just happened. My desire to look for another "new person" in my life had not even begun to register in my brain. But I did promise her that I would soon try to change my outlook on life. But I still needed that thing called *TIME* to heal my wounds and I had not even come close to reaching that point yet.

WHEN would the pain of my loss stop? WHAT would it take to bring me around and back to reality? WHERE was this desire for life and for life's experiences going to present itself to me?

WHO would be the person next in my life to want to be "that special lady"? WHEN would I know that enough time had passed for healing to take place? I knew her presence in my life would *always* be a strong constant! WHY would it be important to try and find a new "partner" in life? Why indeed? WHAT is the point in living when all I felt was a huge, hollow void of any emotional state... of not really caring if I were living or dead? <u>WHY</u> even try again, because I didn't think my heart could take another painful experience or disappointment.

Eventually, I did crawl from the depths of despair, out of sheer loneliness I suspect. I thought I might be able to handle another attempt at looking for a life-partner to share life's ups and downs; to be a team player in the art of living, sharing and caring for one another. This seemed like a good attitude to have arrived at; but being "out of the loop" in the game of relationships for so long, I was totally lost about where or how to begin.

I finally tried "on-line dating"; but the results were horrible! I was either rejected before any type of relationship began or I as the one that did not feel any connection to the other party. So as far as I was concerned... it was a disaster!

<u>WHAT</u> was I doing? <u>WHO</u> did I think I would find merely by chatting "on line" or going out to share a coffee? <u>WHEN</u> would I find a connection to someone to feel something special was happening? <u>WHAT</u> would happen if I just gave up on the whole idea and decided to remain a "loner" in life, and strictly exist as I did before, with my "fond memories" of a special companion? <u>WHO</u>... other than my mother... would really care that I had chosen a life of solitude? <u>WHY</u> had life given me a bowl of "pits" rather than a bowl of "cherries"? <u>WHY</u> was I not worthy of another chance at happiness? <u>WHAT</u> was so wrong with me in the first place?

I did finally realize that living was a full-time job. I remembered a saying that I had once read... *"Enjoy life! It has an expiration date!"* And then I read this... *"Don't worry about old age; it doesn't last that long."*

Remembering these two comments, tended to shed some light on my brain's thinking. It was as though the message was to "keep trying to move forward in life; old age and death will be the end result." What did I really have to lose but a little time and effort in my quest to find that somebody special?

I decided to try once again with the dating site, in my quest for a connection. Hopefully I would take it slow and surely not just "jump in blindly". But life had decided my fate already and had made the decision for me. *ALONE* seemed to be my course on the river of life; but maybe the odd relationship might happen. The dice would roll and I was to be unlucky!

I finally said to myself... *"If it is meant to be that I should be alone, I should accept my fate with grace and just live day by day, taking what may come my way."*

I finally realized that this statement *"you only have* **ONE** *true love in your lifetime"* is true! If others happen to follow, it will never have the same long-lasting effect as your first TRUE love. I had been truly blessed to have found my *TRUE LOVE*... my soul-mate in life and my life's partner.

I had been blessed with all that I could ever have imagined or expected from a meaningful relationship. If it were to happen again, it would be the "exception"... not the normal occurrence to happen in life.

As this had been my quest from the very beginning, I feel it necessary to remind you of the words of the poem that I had included earlier in this book. I wish I had been able to take these words into my existence and live them every day... as much as possible. The whole concept of realizing not to "over reason" the how's and the why's of life. But merely I would have liked to use these words in my daily living. They are profound words!

HANDBOOK OF LIFE
Learn to live with what you have
Feel free to share your love
Always show others you care
Try to speak without harsh words to anyone

Seek happiness throughout your life
Solving problems helps make you strong
Heartache is part of life
Do not be afraid to fail
Success will be your reward

Author: Stephen Paul Tolmie

I read somewhere a great saying that I want to share with you. *"Old age is like a bank account. You withdraw from it what you have already deposited."* So my advice to you is to deposit a lot of happiness in that bank account of memories!

Happiness is something you decide on ahead of time. It is a decision you make every morning when you wake up. You have a choice! You can spend the day in bed recounting the difficulties... the problems... the depressing thoughts. Or you can get out of bed and be thankful for yet another day... a new challenge in another new day. Each day is a gift. As long as you open your eyes, focus on the new day and think about happy memories you have already stored away.

Food for Thought
I remember some sayings from a segment of my life that now comes to my mind that bare repeating.

Do you know why it is so hard to let go?
It's because we "refuse" to let go of the things that make us sad!

Always remember that your present situation
is not your final destination.

The best is yet to come!

The mind replays what the heart cannot delete.

If you are depressed, you are living in the past.
If you are anxious, you are living in the future.
If you are at peace, you are living in the present.

Be someone who makes YOU happy!

One of the hardest decisions you will ever face is
choosing whether to "walk away" or to "try harder".

<u>Five Rules to be Happy</u>
1. Try not to be consumed by hatred.
2. Live life simply.
3. Live within your means.
4. Offer more to others.
5. Accept things that are given freely.

I now realize that in the end, it all boils down to two simple issues in man's two-fold end to life. "One" is to lead man to *Eternal Life,* according to issues revealed to us. The "second" is to guide himself to happiness in the world, according to the teachings of *Life Experiences*... that each one of us has encountered through life.

I have tried my best to take you with me, in my quest for learning about myself and about life itself... including all the issues that had been presented to me in my own life. Hopefully, and in some small way, I have also provided you with some possible solutions that you may be able to hold on to, so that your soul may be at peace... unlike mine.

Perhaps I may have even stimulated some thoughts and some interest in wanting to join me on life's "Merry-Go-Round". Let me ask you this... *"Has your life been all that it should have been? Did you* *have the desire to explore yourself as you read about my trials and tribulations to see if <u>YOU</u> are all that <u>YOU</u> can be?"*

"Why are we here?" The obvious/logical answer that readily comes to mind is, if I was NOT here in the first place, then this question would never have to come to surface to be asked of myself.

I have finally completed the whole circle of my life journey and discovered the answers to the questions I had about myself. Perhaps I may have "over-reasoned" the "whys" and "hows" of life as I looked for answers that were staring me in the face all the time.

I wish I have thought about the poem... *"HANDBOOK OF LIFE"*... early in my life and had been able to apply its message throughout my whole life. It may have been possible that this knowledge might have given me an attempt at becoming a better person and perhaps allowed me to be able to realize some happiness during my life.

<u>WHY</u> was it so hard for me to let go of all the life experiences that had happened to me and that had created so much sadness? <u>WHY</u> was my mind still going over all the pain, time and time again, as my heart relived the misery that I simply can't let go of, and move on?

<u>WHY</u> is it at this point in my life that I reflect on the mistakes and misfortunes and keep reliving them, as if it were yesterday? Why is there no peace in sight? <u>WHERE</u> is this thing called *time* when you finally get "smart enough" about life and all the pitfalls that exist; but realize that now time is running out for you? There is nothing you can do about making any changes to what has already happened.

<u>WHY</u> is the hardest decision that you as a person have to make in your life to choose to carry on after all the times you have been hurt, denied, had your heart broken, never getting that break in life that you needed so desperately and feel like just "ending it"? Do you draw deep within your moral fibre and decide to try harder at living life because

that is the only way to have a longer life-span. You totally realize that "death" is everyone's final end.

WHAT have I truly learned about myself? WHAT have I learned from life's experiences? WHY do I still feel anxious? WHERE was my total life of happiness? WHAT has been my life's purpose? WHO really is the person in this body? WHERE had all the ultimate answers been that I was constantly seeking?

WAS MY WHOLE LIFE'S QUEST
REALLY AS SIMPLE AS THE WORDS
OF A POEM?

"YOU WILL FACE MANY SPEED BUMPS IN YOUR LIFE TIME ....OVERCOMING THEM IS LIVING!.......

About The Author

I was born in the small town of St. Thomas, Ontario, some sixty-six years ago. As in all small towns, everyone knows everyone else's business and their secrets. Consequently there is no end to gossip and rumours to spread around. This can actually aid a writer with some good material if they so choose to incorporate these happenings into their writing. I am just adding this "food for thought" for all the upcoming and future writers to consider.

I worked for the Provincial Government for thirty years and retired at the ripe old age of fifty... as per the government's "eighty point policy"... age plus years of service.

Not knowing what to do with myself and all this *"free time"* on my hands, I became a parking-lot attendant at the local college in London (Fanshawe College) and worked there for ten additional years, speaking with a variety of people. Again, this is a good source for book material if one wanted to pursue "writing a book".

I decided I wanted a new adventure in my life's journey and decided to write because it had always been on my "bucket list" of things I wanted to try before I met my Maker.

Following is a list of some of the books I have written if you have the inclination to check out what I have accomplished on the web.

Now You Have Her... Now You Don't

I wrote this book as a tribute to my wife, who died from cancer in 2004.

That Single Moment

This book deals with the emotions of loving someone special and with the healing process one goes through to "re-start" a personal life.

Estate Planning and Executor's Guide

This "workbook" layout deals with the preparation and organization of your own affairs before death and before you visit your lawyer to prepare your final Will.

Life... Lust... Love

In this book, I tried to "enlighten" the reader about how "inept" I was in the pursuit of someone special to share my life. My "Utopia" was to find someone to go through life's ups and downs with as we built special memories.

Smiles, Poems... Thoughts to Ponder

I hope you enjoy my latest book and that it gives you some smiles, some laughs and some things to think about. It may even help you to avoid some pitfalls and help you enjoy your time on this earth.

Printed in the United States
By Bookmasters